MW01277385

HUMANISTIC BUDDHISM FOR SOCIAL WELL-BEING

An Overview of Grand Master Hsing Yun's Interpretation in Theory and Practice

By

Dr. Ananda W.P. Guruge, Ph.D

BUDDHA'S LIGHT PUBLISHING
LOS ANGELES, U.S.A.

First edition, 2002

Published by Buddha's Light Publishing
3456 South Glenmark Drive
Hacienda Heights, CA 91745.

ISBN 0-971745-2-3
Library of Congress Catalog Number 2002115688

Contents

Author's Note

This brief study of Humanistic Buddhism for social well-being was undertaken at the invitation of Fo Guang Shan Buddhist Order. It provided me with a long-awaited opportunity to present Humanistic Buddhism, as conceived and interpreted by Venerable Grand Master Dr. Hsing Yun, from two standpoints:

- its place in promoting and establishing the universality of Buddhism, and
- its relevance and effectiveness in the modern world.

I am deeply indebted to Venerable Grand Master Dr. Hsing Yun for enabling me to study and understand his concept of Humanistic Buddhism in theory and practice, to Dr. Naichen Chen, President of Hsi Lai University, Los Angeles County, California, USA for his kind assistance in every way, to my colleagues and friends Roger Schmidt, James Santucci, Tom Graham and Richard Kimball for reading the first draft and making useful suggestions, Connie Kuang for liaison with the Fo Guang Shan Buddhist Order and Lejun Bu for preparing the text for print.

HUMANISTIC BUDDHISM FOR SOCIAL WELL-BEING

Introduction

Grand Master Hsing Yun's Introduction to Humanistic Buddhism

Venerable Dr. Hsing Yun is the Grand Master of the Fo Guang Shan Buddhist Order, the 48th Patriarch of Linji Chan tradition, and the foremost Chinese scholar-monk of our times. He has been impressed, since his adolescence, with humanism as the all-pervading characteristic of the teachings of the Buddha. He has devoted a life-time of study, research, contemplation, discussion, and teaching to clarify and elaborate the philosophical concepts inherent in Buddhism and their practical implications. The ultimate result of this effort is the identification of core teachings of the Buddha, which are relevant and immediately applicable to life in this modern world. He calls these teachings Humanistic Buddhism (*Renjian Fojiao*). He sees in it an enormous potential for social well-being and individual advancement.

In re-emphasizing the humanistic overtones of the Buddha's teachings, the Grand Master had an exemplar in his own spiritual predecessor, Huineng (638-713), the Sixth Patriarch of the Chan School, who said,

Buddhism is in the world;

> It is not realized apart from the world.
> Seeking enlightenment apart from the world
> Is like looking for horns on a hare....
> Good friends, if you want to put this into practice, you can do it at home — it doesn't depend on being in a monastery. Being able to practice at home is like someone of the East whose mind is good.
>
> (Thomas Cleary [Tr.], 1998, p. 23)

In 1946, when he was just 19 years old, Grand Master Hsing Yun met a senior enthusiast who was also convinced of Patriarch Huineng's vision of Buddhism as an integral part of human life in this very world. The Grand Master of Fo Guang Shan tells us about his meeting with Master Taixu:

> "In July 1946, Venerable Taixu presided over a routine lecture of the Chinese Buddhist Association. I was fortunate to have a chance to attend it. Venerable Taixu excitedly called on us, saying, 'We must establish the characteristics of Humanistic Buddhism!'
>
> I was enlightened by Master Taixu's words. Now I see the meaning of the following:
>
> > 'The Buddha was born in the human world.
> > He practiced the cultivation in the human world
> > And he became enlightened in the world.
> > He lectured in the world.
> > His whole life embodied the characteristics of Humanistic Buddhism.
> > For forty-nine years, he offered more than 300 lectures.
> > He did not speak to gods or devils, or to hells, or to those who are born as animals.
> > He taught dharma to people.'"
>
> (*P'umen — Universal Gate Monthly — No. 3, 1999, pp.4-11*)

Master Taixu's Concept of Humanistic Buddhism

Master Taixu's insights had been sharpened by his incisive observation of the situation of Buddhism in China and his in-depth review of other forms of Buddhism elsewhere in Asia. The comparisons that Master Taixu made are significant and need to be highlighted to understand his message which inspired a young generation to act. As regards Buddhism in China, he identified the following as needing urgent reform and action:

1. The overriding focus on the theory of self-cultivation and its sequel in the isolation of Buddhists from society;
2. "Empty talk of Mahāyāna theories and the neglect of practice" — "a missing link between theory and practice."
3. The failure to be inspired by the great spirit of compassionate love in Buddhism for action toward social well-being; and
4. The need to orient Buddhists to serve the nation, the state, and the world.

Master Taixu had been himself inspired by what he had seen in Southern Buddhism as taught and practiced in Myanmar (Burma), Thailand and Sri Lanka (Ceylon). He observed that Buddhism in these countries had become "the people's religion." He was particularly impressed with Sri Lanka. He noted that

(i) Great efforts are made to study the doctrines and to observe precepts by monastics as well as the laity;

(ii) Not only Buddhists from Myanmar and Thailand but also scholars doing research in Southern Buddhism and Pali language from various parts of the world come there to study Buddhism; and

(iii) Buddhists are engaged in many causes such as social welfare, culture, education and so forth and thus benefit the state, society and "even broad masses in the world" — "marking a great spirit of compassionate love in Buddhism."

He expressed his enthusiasm saying, "Though Buddhism in Sri Lanka is generally considered to be Theravāda, it is indeed the practice of Mahāyāna Buddhism." (*Tai Xu Dashi Quanshu*, Vol. 35, pp. 26-30, translated and quoted in Darui Long, 2000, p. 64)

It is thus very clear that Master Taixu's concept of "Humanistic Buddhism" was a platform for reform action for the conversion of Buddhism in China *from* its isolation as a path of self-cultivation, practiced by a limited few, *to* a universal religion dedicated to a broad spectrum of initiatives for human well-being. Considering the cataclysmic changes which were taking place in China in mid-twentieth century, his campaign was timely. It had to be parochial and China-centered. It was action-oriented. Master Taixu had little need for a conceptual or philosophical basis for his action for bringing Buddhism literally and metaphorically from the mountains to the living society.

Where Master Taixu and Grand Master Hsing Yun Differ

To the young, fertile, and vigorous mind of Hsing Yun, Taixu's call for a humanistic form of Buddhism had a wider meaning. He embarked on study and investigation. His search was for the inner essence of Buddhism in its diverse manifestations. How actually can Buddhism serve humanity? What contents in the Śākyamuni Buddha's teachings highlight service to humankind? Where should one look for exemplars and guidance in evolving a form of humanistic Buddhism? The search had to be on his own. The inspirer of the new line of investigation, namely Master Taixu, died just a year after the memorable meeting of 1946.

Thus Hsing Yun had no opportunity to benefit directly from the insights and aspirations of Taixu who could, under different circumstances, have been Grand Master Hsing Yun's mentor and teacher. But that was not to be.[1] As a result, Grand Master Hsing

[1] Richard L. Kimball's following statement regarding Master Tai Xu's influence on Grand Master Hsing Yun needs clarification in the light of Master Tai Xu's death in 1947 and Grand Master Hsing Yun's own independent and innovative exploration of humanism in Buddhism: "The Grand Master read most of his writings and heard him lecture on a number of occasions... He was both a role model and mentor to Grand

Yun's research and contemplation, though inspired initially by Master Taixu's enthusiasm, had to be based on his own devices. In it the young scholar-activist had some significant advantages. As a result, he could surpass the elder master in scope, complexity and operational diversity of what each called Humanistic Buddhism.

Their major difference has been in outlook, intellectual emphasis and mode of action. Master Taixu saw weaknesses in Chinese Buddhism vis-à-vis modern science, education and development. He would urge his countrymen to look up to Christian models and emulate the socially engaged Christian missionary:

> "The Christians devote themselves to advancing the general social welfare. They propagate their teachings by practicing altruism. This is something of significance and we may adopt it."
>
> (Quoted in Darui Long, 2000, p. 63)

On another occasion, Master Taixu urged Buddhists to support the Government in its war efforts "to build a powerful nation." His political agitation earned him a less-than-complimentary description as a "political monk." It is true that he upheld Mahāyāna Buddhism and his advocacy on its behalf was genuine and sincere. But when he aimed at social well-being of the masses, he saw no contradiction in urging that the Chinese should adopt or emulate Christianity for the sake of its modernizing influences in science and education. Of course, he had a knack to be incisive in his statements. In the same predominantly Christian assembly, Master Taixu urged the West to adopt Buddhism to rationalize its thinking. (For details, see Darui Long 2000-1)

As regards the mode of action, Master Taixu was an agitator in building public opinion. He stirred up people and certain good results followed, like schools and educational development. Just before his death he lamented his failure saying that he was "good at

---

Master Hsing Yun."(*Kimball, 2000, p.12*) After a discussion, Kimball amended it to read as follow: "The Grand Master had read some of his [Tai Xu's] writings and heard his lecture on at least one occasion. He was influenced by both Master Tai Xu's teachings and determination. He was one role model for Grand Master Hsing Yun."

theory and poor in practice;" that he fell out with the conservatives in the mainstream; and that he failed in leading the Buddhists in their endeavors for reform and advancement (Darui Long 2000, p. 65).

Grand Master Hsing Yun's Original and Innovative Strategy

In contrast to Master Taixu, Grand Master Hsing Yun developed his strategy around learning and scholarship, research and contemplation, systematic planning and deliberate but cautious activism. He was a visionary with his head above the clouds but his feet secured firmly on the ground. He chose to appeal to the intellect of the people rather than to their emotions. He acquired knowledge for himself but readily shared it with others using every available opportunity and modality. He taught; he wrote; he spoke; and he broadcast. In every way he captured the attention of his audience, whether in a modest class-room or in a radio talk reaching thousands or in millions of households where people switched on their televisions to his transmissions on Humanistic Buddhism.

In all his communications Grand Master Hsing Yun has been self-searching. He reviews his life experiences to illustrate how Humanistic Buddhism affected his thinking and actions. He draws lessons from things, which happened to him and to others. He finds inspiration from whatever source where humanity had risen above pettiness and disharmony to kindness, compassion and peaceful co-existence. He distills his brand of Buddhism in action through his concern for the well-being of every man, woman and child throughout the world.

Grand Master Hsing Yun's intellectual commitment has no boundaries. He has a message for the scholar and the activist; the passive contemplator and the aggressive agitator; the self-effacing monastic and the most worldly seeker of pleasure. This unique universality of intellectual approach, thus, gives him pride of place within his own religious order. Millions of adherents to his teachings on all continents of the world look up to his guidance. He is their acknowledged leader, mentor, guide and friend. The power of his message and the universality of intellectual approach has earned him respect and influence far beyond the reaches of Buddhist traditions. No Buddhist leader of modern times has risen to such heights of popular acceptance *solely* by dint of his own personal effort and achievements.

Breadth of Vision and Universality of Thought

What Grand Master Hsing Yun has gained by his universal intellectual appeal is further enhanced by the sheer depth of his scholarship. He began with the known. That included the entire Buddhist literature in Chinese, in which the Mahāyāna sūtras were predominant. He studied the traditions of his own school, writing masterful commentaries on the *Platform Sūtra of Huineng* and the *Amitābha Sūtra*. He grasped the essence of Chan and reached his own conclusions on Pure Land as present to be actualized in this very life.

He explored through the *Diamond Sūtra* the way to become a Bodhisattva and perfected his understanding of wisdom and emptiness. He grasped the significance of the six Pāramitas as a foundation of Buddhist ethics. He analyzed *Mahāprajñāpāramitā Śāstra* for its crucial teachings on the perfection of wisdom, and found in *Vimalakīrtinirdeśa-sūtra* a perennial appeal to righteousness.

In *Yogācārabhūmisūtra* and *Karmavibhangasūtra*, he found the essence of Buddhist morality. So to him were other texts like *Saddharmapuṇḍarīkasūtra*, *Avataṃsakasūtra*, *Śūrangamasūtra*, *Sukhāvatisūtra*, *Saddharmasmṛtyupasthānasūtra*, *Mahāratnakūṭa*, *Vijñaptimātratāsiddhiśāstra*, *Samantabhadrotsahanaparivartasūtra*, *Sutrataparipṛcchasūtra*, *Abhiniṣkramaṇasūtra*, *Mahāyānaśraddhoppādasūtra*, *Kuśalamūlasaṃgrahasūtra*, *Fo Shou Bei Sūtra*, - a veritable treasurehouse of insights and information from which he extracted the essence of Buddhism.

From these, he proceeded to the Āgama Sūtras to read and understand Śākyamuni Buddha's teachings to human beings. He became as well-versed in the *Ekottarāgama*, the *Saṃyuktāgama* and many sūtras of the *Dīrghāgama* as in Mahāyānasūtras.

The wider his reading and study, the more profound was his appreciation of Buddhism as an enormously rich and varied philosophical heritage of humanity. In his books and speeches, he would quote from all traditions: from *Dhammapada* and *Sigālovādasutta*, from *Upāsakaśīla* and *Mahāparinirvāṇasūtra* in the same breath as he cited the *Sūtra in Forty-two Sections* and the *Five-Part Vinaya*. While many spoke of the importance of benefiting from the diversity of Buddhist traditions — especially from their literary masterpieces — Grand Master Hsing Yun blazed a new trail. He has become the symbol of unity for all Buddhist traditions — a crowning success of his undaunting efforts which the World Fellowship of Buddhists has recognized by electing him the Honorary President for life.

His books and speeches demonstrate the unity of Buddhist concepts and ideals. This unity becomes clearer as Grand Master Hsing Yun marshals most skillfully the wide array of diverse Buddhist scriptures to highlight the humanistic foundation of the Buddha's unique Path of Deliverance.

Grand Master Hsing Yun takes us back to the Buddha, the man, who taught human beings on the banks of the river Gangā — the very origin of the ethical idealism which we call Buddhism.

Quintessence of Grand Master Hsing Yun's Insights

The most recent declaration of the quintessence of Grand Master Hsing Yun's insights on Humanistic Buddhism is contained in his message to the inaugural session of the First International Conference on Humanistic Buddhism, held at Hsi Lai University in California, USA, on December 13, 1999. In it he said,

> "Buddhism is a religion that belongs to all sentient beings no matter who they are or where they are. No one is ever to be left out of its reach. Only through dynamic cooperation between the Sangha and the lay followers, between the scholar and the student, will we ever be able to spread the Dharma to all who have a need of it.
>
> In Buddhism, the human realm is the most important realm of all. The human realm is the realm where great transformations can occur. Not only

have all the Buddhas in the universe achieved enlightenment in this realm, but this also is where great sages and great Bodhisattvas appear to preach the Dharma. Bodhidharma, Faxian, Xuanzang and many others underwent great hardships solely for the good of sentient beings living in the human realm.

It is a real pity that so many Buddhists, especially when they first begin to practice, place so much emphasis on long retreats and on liberating themselves from the cycle of birth and death. These are important concerns, but remember, no one is going to achieve liberation from the cycle of birth and death if he has not figured out how to live as a human being in the human realm.

All of us must live fully, virtuously and compassionately in this world before we can ever expect to transcend anything. In the past, Buddhism too often was characterized by passivity and inactivity. Buddhists too often were content to "follow conditions" and not create them themselves. Without a vision of our future, Buddhism will continue to languish in its cocoon, and by doing that, fundamentally contradict some of its most basic principles. As we draw to the beginning of the 21st century and the third millennium — only eighteen days away from today — I believe it is essential that we create a vibrant vision of the future of Buddhism in this world.

The world is changing quickly. To grasp these changes and use them for our good, we must fully comprehend the inter-workings of societies, science, economics, governments and the environment. If Buddhism is to develop as a viable religion in the world, it must adapt itself to the conditions, which are present in this world. Every choice we make of the future of Buddhism should be founded on clear reasoning and good intentions. The path of the Arhant has its Four Directions and Four Fruits, while the Bodhisattva Way of Mahāyāna is divided into fifty-two detailed stages. These details and divisions show the importance that Buddhism places on clarity of vision and good planning.

Humanistic Buddhism emphasizes our treatment of other people above everything else. No one can ever expect to come into full awareness of the Bodhi mind if they do not know how to treat other people with compassion, respect and unfailing kindness. Meditation and chanting are not means to escape this earth. The concentration, wisdom, peace and joy that we find in meditation are skills that should be applied in this world. We should use them whenever we deal with others.

All Buddhists are living representatives of Śākyamuni Buddha, his teachings, and his compassion. Our basic faith comes from the Buddha himself. His teachings and his life are an example of truth, virtue, wisdom and perseverance. The Dharma is based on a reliance on our own innermost Buddha nature and the wisdom of our own inherent Bodhi mind. Through unity and compassion we will succeed in bringing Buddhism to all world's people."

In the ensuing chapters, each element highlighted by Grand Master Hsing Yun in this concise statement will be examined in depth with special reference to Early Buddhism. My aim is to show how the teachings of Śākyamuni, the historical Buddha (circa 563-483 BCE)[2], as recorded in the Pali Tipiṭaka of Southern Buddhism

[2] A recent trend among Western scholars of Buddhist Studies like Heinz Bechert of Germany and Richard Gombrich of Britain to bring down the date of the Buddha by

and the Chinese Āgama Sūtras of Northern Buddhism, converge in underscoring the profound religious and philosophical concepts on which Grand Master Hsing Yun has formulated the theory and practice of Humanistic Buddhism for social well-being.

---

about a hundred years has not led to any convincing conclusion as they ignore (a) the Pali sources which agree with the Purāṇas and Xuanzang as regards two Aśokas (Kālāśoka and Dharmāśoka) and (b) the intervening royal dynasties from Bimbisāra, (the Buddha's contemporary) to Candragupta, the founder of the Mauryan dynasty.

The Universality of Buddhism

All Sentient Beings Without Exception (Pāṇabhūtā anavasesā)

"Buddhism is a religion that belongs to all sentient beings no matter who they are or where they are. No one is ever to be left out of its reach," says Grand Master Hsing Yun.

Śākyamuni Buddha spoke of universes without end or limit (*anantam aparimāṇam*) and sentient beings were said to exist everywhere. He was described as a teacher of gods and humans (*satthādevamanussānam*) and his compassion extended to innumerable universes. In an attempt to encompass beings to whom we are counseled to direct our thoughts of loving kindness, he listed them as

> Whatsoever life exists —
> Weak or strong without exception,
> Long and huge, medium, short,
> Miniscule as an atom or fat,
> Seen or unseen,
> Living nearby or far away,
> Born or seeking to be born

(Suttanipāta I, 8)

So comprehensive is this listing that no one is excluded. Just as they are to be recipients of our friendship and compassion, they are also in need of the Buddha's message of deliverance.

Doctrine of Three Marks or Signs of Existence

All sentient beings have one thing in common. Wherever they be — whether in Pure States or Brahma worlds with or without form, in celestial abodes in the sensual sphere, in human existence or in other states as animals, spirits and so forth — they are subjected to the ineluctable reality of impermanence, transitoriness or transience. All beings are born, exist for long or short periods, and eventually die to be born again in the relentless *saṃsāra* (the cycle of birth and death). In *Anattalakkhaṇasutta*, the second sermon of his mission to his one-time companions in fasting and penance, the Buddha chose to present the characteristic of impermanence or *Anicca* (Skt. *Anitya*) as the foundation of his theory of Three Signs, Marks or Signata (*tilakkhaṇa*) of Existence.[3]

Where only impermanence and change reigned, there could be no predictable tomorrow. Nothing could be as one wanted or planned. One had no control or power over change. The mightiest falls from the highest of glory and the strongest becomes subject to debilitating sickness and decay. In such a situation of flux, one finds no satisfaction or happiness. As the Buddha argued, in such a state of impermanence and change, there could only be dissatisfaction, misery and suffering. That to him was the second reality of existence, namely *Dukkha* (translatable as unsatisfactoriness, misery, and suffering). This again applies to all beings wherever they are.

In spite of these two Signs or Marks, which characterized existence, an illusion of self enabled beings to be selfish and self-centered, conceited and self-satisfied. In the midst of miserable transience, what a being believed to be his permanent, unchanging self could have no reality. The reality, the Buddha perceived, was

---

[3] The concept of *Three Seals of Dharma* in Chinese sources is somewhat different from this doctrine. The Three Seals are Impermanence, No-self, and Nirvāṇa.

the absence of a self which could proclaim "This is mine, this is I and this is my Self." The third sign was designated by the term *Anatta* (No-Self).

What the Buddha underscored with his doctrine of Three Marks or Signs was the futility and emptiness of existence. It was his conviction that attachment to an illusory Self as though it were permanent and unchanging caused dissatisfaction and suffering. There he found the cause of misery, which was the lot of every sentient being.

Doctrine of Four Noble Truths

A few days earlier, the Buddha had delivered his very first sermon to the same audience. The *Dhammacakkappavattanasutta* (the discourse of turning the wheel of Dharma or Doctrine) began with what was foremost in his mind when he met his comrades-in-austerity. They had abandoned the ascetic Buddha-to-be when he gave up austere fasting and took to a more normal life. So he extolled the importance of the Middle Path which avoided both extremes of luxury or self-indulgence and of painful penance or self-mortification.

From there he went straight to a discourse of *Dukkha*, which he presented as the First Noble Truth because it was true in respect of every sentient being. Using situations which were clear and self-explanatory, he defined *Dukkha* as the pain and misery one experienced with

- birth[4]
- decay or old age
- disease
- death
- association with the unloved or the unpleasant

[4] Birth is conceived as suffering as the other forms of misery and suffering are consequent to one's birth. Philosophically the explanation is that birth results in death and that in rebirth. So did the Buddha describe a person who had reached the supreme bliss of Nibbāṇa through enlightenment as "never returning to lie in a womb again" (*na hi jātu gabbhaseyyaṃ punareti* — (*Khuddakapāṭha: Mettasutta*, also *Suttanipāta I, 8*).

- separation from the loved or the pleasant
- not getting what one desires, and
- in brief, the five groups of attachment (namely, form, feeling, perception, mental formations and consciousness).

Already in this definition of *Dukkha*, the Buddha had expressed his concept of a sentient being as an amalgam of five aggregates or *khandhas* (Sanskrit *Skandhas*). As is explained later, a being is comprised of the physical form and four mental or psychological functions. When this teaching is brought in line with the Third Sign of Selflessness or *Anatta*, the resulting definition of a sentient being is "**a grouping of the physical body and the psychological functions of feeling, perception, mental formations such as recognition, memory and latent tendencies and the like and consciousness but without a permanent or unchanging self or soul which could say 'This is mine; This is I; This is my Self'**." A sentient being is subject to suffering and misery as each aggregate is inclined towards attachment (*upādāna*) because of self-illusion.

Though already hinted, the Buddha elaborated the concept of attachment as the Second Noble Truth — the Cause of Suffering:

> It is craving which produces rebirth, accompanied by passionate clinging, seeking delight now here and now there. That is the craving for sensuous pleasure, for becoming and for extinction.

If the Buddha taught *Dukkha* and its cause, he would have been another philosopher expounding his own world-view. He was no philosopher even though he certainly contributed to the development of signal philosophical concepts and views. He renounced the comforts of his palace and the pleasures of royalty to seek answers to the miseries of existence of every sentient being. It took him six years of study and contemplation, experimentation and austerities. But eventually he did discover the end to suffering. Presenting the end of suffering as the Third Noble Truth, he said,

> It is the complete eradication of craving, the withdrawal from it, its renunciation and over-throwal, liberation from it and non-attachment to it.

He called it simply *Nirodha* (cessation) in the *Dhamma-cakkappavattana-sutta* but later elaborated it as *Nibbāṇa* — a state of tranquillity, peace, bliss, protection, security, stability, endless-ness, immortality, and emancipation. *Nibbāṇa* results from the eradication of craving, clinging, lust, hatred and ignorance. It is attained with incomparable supreme enlightenment. *Nibbāṇa*, the Buddha stressed, is to be experienced in this life. It is not within the grasp of mere logical inference (*atakkāvacara*).

Liberation from suffering and misery is within the reach of every sentient being. It is not the preserve of a privileged few. Of course, one has to achieve it by one's own efforts. The Buddhas were only there to point the way:

> The task has to be accomplished by you and you alone
> The Buddhas are but teachers (*akkhātāro*).
>
> (*Dhammapada, 276*)

The Fourth Noble Truth is that way. He called it the "Path leading to the end of suffering" (*Dukkhanirodhagāmiṇīpaṭipadā*). We shall return to an analysis of this Path. In the meantime, let us look at another doctrine of Early Buddhism which once again shows the Buddha's preoccupation with suffering and misery and with the way out of it.

Doctrine of Twelve-Stage Dependent Origination (Paṭiccasamu-ppāda)

Tradition says that the Buddha thought out the formulation of Dependent Origination during his first week of meditation at the Bodhi Tree of Gaya after his enlightenment. It begins with a taxonomy of *Dukkha* as comprising

- aging (*jarā*= decay)
- death (*maraṇa*)
- sorrow (*soka*)
- lamentation (*parideva*)

- pain (*dukkha*)
- grief (*domanassa*)
- despair (*upāyāsā*)

These are termed "the whole mass of suffering." Such suffering which all sentient beings share arises from *Birth* (*jāti*) or, more precisely, rebirth. Birth or rebirth is conditioned by the process of *Becoming* (*bhava*) and that in turn by *Clinging* (*upādāna*). Clinging is conditioned by *Craving* (*taṇhā*), which in turn is produced by *Feeling* (*vedanā*). Feeling originates with *Contact with the external world* (*phassa*) while such contact occurs through the *six sense bases* (eye, ear, nose, tongue, body and mind). The analysis goes further by explaining the Six Sense Bases as a product of the *Mental and Physical phenomena* (*nāma-rūpa*). These in turn are produced by Consciousness (*viññāna*) which is generated by rebirth-producing *Mental formations* or *Volitional activities* (sankhāra). Volitional activities are conditioned by *Ignorance* or *Non-knowledge (avijjā).*

In the doctrine of Dependent Origination, thus, *ignorance* or *non-knowledge* (*avijjā*) is the primary cause of suffering of sentient beings. It is the non-realization of the true nature of existence as stated in Three Marks or Signs that prompts one to think in terms of a permanent and unchanging Self. This ego-centric view of Self (*sakkāyadiṭṭhi*) is the root of craving, clinging, lust, hatred, and delusion.

The Buddha explains in this manner that the basic foundation for the ending of suffering is *wisdom* (*paññā*) which is the antithesis of ignorance or non-knowledge (*avijjā*). Once *avijjā* is eradicated, no more rebirth-producing mental activities arise and the progressive chain reaction culminates in the end of suffering.

Path of Liberation

Thus in diverse ways has Śākyamuni Buddha expressed his concern with suffering and its end. It was in fact his fundamental concern. When he was once asked what his message was, he replied, "I teach suffering and the ending of suffering." He engaged himself in a strenuous mission as a religious teacher because of his compassion to save sentient beings from suffering and misery. It is said that he began each day with a period of deep compassionate meditation (*karuṇāsamāpatti*), surveying the world to see who needed his help. It is thus that he went in search of a ruthless murderer who would have otherwise killed his own mother.

Within four months of enlightenment, when he had just sixty disciples, the Buddha told them,

> "Monastics, go forth. Go forth on a mission for the good of the many, for the happiness of the many, with compassion towards the world, for the benefit, the welfare and the happiness of men and gods. Let not two of you go the same way. Preach to them, O Monastics, the doctrine, lovely in the beginning, lovely in the middle, lovely in the end and full of meaning and distinctive characteristics. Proclaim to them pure and complete Higher Life. I myself am proceeding to Uruvela to preach the doctrine."

(Mv. 1, 21)

The key sentiment is "compassion towards the world, for the benefit, the welfare and the happiness of humans and gods."

The Path to end suffering which the Buddha discovered and the many discourses, debates, discussions and poetic compositions, through which his messages for the benefit of sentient beings were expressed, constitute *Buddhism*. One may object to the use of "Buddhism" as a term to describe the multifaceted teachings of a supremely wise and resourceful teacher like the Buddha. He preached nothing dogmatic. He urged his audiences not to accept things simply because they were in their books or were a part of the family tradition or were taught by a teacher they liked. He wanted everyone to think and think for oneself asking the basic question, "Is what is preached to the benefit, welfare and happiness of the many?" (*Kālāmasutta, Anguttaranikāya* I, pp. 188 ff.)

He sought no converts to his faith or point of view and specifically said so in *Udumbarikasīhanādasutta*. To those who were convinced by his teachings and wished to follow him, he said further,

1. Let him who is your teacher be your teacher still;
2. Let that which is your rule be your rule still;
3. Let that which is your mode of livelihood be so still;
4. Let those points in your doctrines which are wrong and reckoned as wrong by those in your community, remain so still for you;
5. Let those points in your doctrines which are good, reckoned to be good by those in your community, remain so still.

(D. 25: *Udumbarikā Sīhanādasutta*)

Irrespective of what one believed in or practiced, one could follow the teachings of the Buddha. He had all sentient beings as his audience. Grand Master Hsing Yun rightly says that the Buddha's teachings belong to all sentient beings and no one is ever to be left out of its reach.

Spreading the Dharma

Targeting All Who Have Need of the Dharma

It is the view of Grand Master Hsing Yun that only through dynamic cooperation between the Sangha and the lay followers, between the scholar and the student, will we ever be able to spread the Dharma to all who have need of it.

Śākyamuni Buddha intended his teachings to reach everybody. We noted how he commenced his missionary movement when he had just sixty disciples. He himself returned to Gaya to embark on a missionary role which lasted over four decades (45 years according to Southern Buddhism and 49 years according to Northern Buddhism). Though the target was each and everyone, the Buddha was realistic about individual differences. Some were more inclined to accept the discipline he demanded. Others were not. Either they had responsibilities and obligations, which they could not set aside, or liberation was not their priority.[5] Some had

[5] At a speech delivered by me in January 1974 at the World Fellowship of Buddhists in Bangkok, Thailand, I said, "If somebody were to come today and say 'I can take you straight to Nibbāṇa this very minute,' I think most of us will have lots of excuses to give." Some will say, "Can't I wait till my daughter gets married?" Another

fulfilled the pre-requisites for liberation over life times and were said to possess *upanissaya* (i.e. sufficing condition or qualification for enlightenment).

The recognition of individual differences enabled the Buddha to tailor and graduate his teachings to suit each person and his or her level of intellectual development. His method of instruction was gradual, going from the known to the unknown and from the simple to the difficult. He illustrated it with several analogies. As the sandy beach slopes into the ocean gradually without pitfalls, cracks or crags and the depth of water increases steadily and not abruptly, so was knowledge to be given to a student — gradually increasing in depth and complexity. (*Udāna*, V, 5) An accountant would teach a student counting from one the unity, two the duality, three the trinity and so forth. So was all teaching to be done starting with the basics. The taming of a wild elephant was another metaphor. Here a well-trained elephant was engaged to take away the wild ways of the captured animal and get it used to the ways of the village. The educational principle involved in this comparison relates to unlearning the unwanted and learning from peers. The Buddha's overall approach to instruction was through methodically progressive exercises. (Guruge, 1982, pp. 30-31)

What we had discussed in the earlier chapter shows that the Buddha had a well-planned curriculum. The ultimate goal of instruction was to lead the learner (*sekha*) to the level where no more learning was necessary (*asekha*, literally, no more a learner). This stage was reached when one exerted oneself diligently and steadfastly and reached perfect enlightenment whether as a Buddha, a Pacceka Buddha or a Śrāvaka.[6] The Path leading to this stage

---

might say, "Can't I wait till my son gets a job?" "Can't I wait till I have finished my assignment?" We have our own preferred times when it comes even to the ultimate goal because of our attachment to things here and now." — *Gems of Buddhist Wisdom*, Buddhist Missionary Society, Kuala Lumpur, 1983/1996, p. 332.

[6] Early Buddhism recognizes that enlightenment could be achieved in three ways: as a *Buddha* (who becomes enlightened by his own effort and leads others to liberation); as a *Pacceka* (Private or Silent) *Buddha* (who becomes enlightened by his own effort but does not lead others to liberation); or as a *Śrāvaka* (disciple, who gains enlightenment on being instructed by a Buddha or his teachings. All three had

where the entire mass of suffering ended had to be learned and practiced. As he said about the Four Noble Truths, *dukkha* had to be known and understood, its cause eradicated, the end of *dukkha* attained, and the Path leading to it practiced.

The Buddha was a pragmatist. He was convinced that one needs to know what is knowable and directly utilizable by oneself. Knowledge for knowledge's sake was not his goal. In fact, he ridiculed those who acquired too much of even the knowledge of the Dhamma: he called them cowherds who tend cattle for other people's use:

> Though much he recites the Sacred Texts but acts not in accordance with the Teaching, he shares not the blessings of a recluse, like a cowherd counting others' cattle.
>
> Though little he recites the Sacred Texts but acts in accordance with the Teaching, and forsaking lust, hatred, and ignorance, truly knowing, with mind totally freed, clinging for naught here and hereafter, he shares the blessings of a recluse.
>
> (Dp. 19, 20)

He had also a metaphor for those who were attached to learning even the Dhamma beyond its practical objective: they were compared to a person who makes a raft to cross a river and, out of gratitude to it, carries it on his head, hampering his journey beyond. (M. 22 — *Alagaddūpamasutta*)

His pragmatic choice of the essential from interesting but unneeded knowledge is conveyed by the parable of the wounded man:

> "If a man were pierced through by a poisoned arrow and his friends, companions and relatives called in a surgeon and the man should say, 'I will not have this arrow pulled out until I know who the man is who wounded me, whether he is a Kṣatriya,

---

the epithet of *Arahant*, meaning "worthy". It is in Mahāyāna literature that *Arahant* is equated to *Śrāvaka*.

> a Brahman, a citizen or a servant' or else he should say, 'I will not have this arrow pulled out until I know who the man is that wounded me, whether he is tall or short or of medium height' verily such a man would die before he could sufficiently get to know all this."

(M. 63 — *Cūlamālunkyasutta*)

He thus discouraged his disciples from looking for or speculating on the beginning of things, the creation, the creator and similar issues. His advice was to be concerned with what is at hand — **the present moment**, when one thing was clear: impermanence and change reigned supreme and the result was suffering and misery, attended by aging, death, sorrow, lamentation, pain, grief and despair; no being was there in such a context who could claim "This is mine. This is I. This is my Self."

On another occasion, the Buddha listed ten questions on which he chose to be silent:

1. Is the Universe eternal?
2. Or is it not eternal?
3. Is the Universe finite?
4. Or is it infinite?
5. Is the soul the same as the body?
6. Are the soul and the body different?
7. Does the Buddha exist after death?
8. Does he cease to exist after death?
9. Does he both exist and cease to exist after death?
10. Does he both not exist and not cease to exist?

(D. 9 — *Po ṭṭhapādasutta*, M. 63 — *Cūlamālunkyasutta*, S. XXXIII, 1-55 *Vacchagottasaṃyutta*)

An anecdote concerning Śākyamuni Buddha's closest and most generous lay devotee and benefactor, Anāthapiṇḍika, relates to differentiated subject matter. It shows that each learner was taught according to his or her immediate needs. Anāthapiṇḍika was a regular visitor to the Buddha and his monastic disciples at the monastery he had donated. He had heard many discourses and participated in discussions. But when Śāriputra and Ānanda preached to him at his death-bed, he was surprised. He had never heard these doctrines ever before. They explained, "Such talks on the Dhamma are not given to the white-clothed laity: they are given to those gone forth from the house life" (M. 143). Another clear instance is where the subject-matter — in this case the technique and object of meditation — was designed according to temperament of the learner. Out of forty different instructions (*kammaṭṭhāna*) the most appropriate was to be chosen.

Four conclusions are to be drawn from what the Buddha and his disciples said and did as regards the spread of the Dharma:

(1) The Dharma had to be brought to each and sundry as all beings had a need of it. (No two were to take the same route, the Buddha advised the first batch of sixty missionary monks. That emphasizes how widely he wanted the Dhamma to be disseminated).

(2) Teaching had to be according to each person's capacity to learn. An enormous body of textual knowledge is not needed to lead the Buddha's way of life.

(3) Differentiated subject-matter out of the Buddha's doctrines and teachings had to be carefully selected to suit each individual's learning needs. Monastics and the laity were taught differently. An individual's needs, temperament and capacity determined what aspects of the Dhamma was relevant and useful to him or her.

(4) The subject-matter for the laity was determined in terms of what was directly applicable to life as a householder.

The Sangha — A Society of Ideal Educators

The word Sangha, meaning a community of monastics, is older than Buddhism as are terms like *Śramaṇa* (*Samaṇa*), *Muni*, *Yati*, *Bhikṣu* which referred to monastics. While monastics belonged to an organized Order or Community, there were others who were ascetics or recluses (*tāpasas*) who pursued their own forms of austere penances or religious observances. Close to the time of

Śākyamuni Buddha, Jina Mahāvīra, the founder of Jainism, had his Order of monks and nuns called the Sangha.

The Buddha thus adopted for his purposes an age-old institution (some trace its presence to 3000 BCE). But he made a number of significant innovations, which facilitated its survival and vitality for twenty-six centuries. The Sangha was conceived as a group motivated by a common objective, subscribing to a common way of life, and guided by a common set of rules and regulations. As a self-regulatory body which constantly renewed itself through recruitment, the Sangha evolved itself over several decades in the Buddha's life-time to have its own code of conduct. The Vinaya or Discipline is preserved in all three traditions of Buddhism (Southern, Northern and Vajrayāna) in remarkable uniformity. It comprises not only rules of monastic discipline but a most impressive array of regulations on dress and food, table etiquette and social manners, and advice on matters ranging from personal hygiene to disposal of human waste.

The Sangha had elements of social organization which the Buddha considered to be ideal and beneficial. It was a community of equals whatever be the social, economic or cultural background from which the individual members came:

> Just as waters of various rivers lost their identity when they flowed into the ocean, persons of different castes lost their previous social identities in the Sangha.
>
> (Guruge, 2000, p. 100)

Precedence among members for practical purposes such as receiving alms was determined by the seniority in membership (i.e. from the time of ordination). Similarly each member was equal economically since he or she renounced all worldly possessions. The very term *bhikṣu* or its feminine form *bhikṣuṇi*, meaning a mendicant or one who begged for food, reflected the vow of poverty to which every member adhered.

Within the Sangha, too, everything was held in common for the use of the community as a whole. No one had any right of inheritance or bequest. At death, even the meager personal belongings devolved to the Sangha to be allotted to a deserving monk or nun. Every donation was accepted and held in the name of the Sangha. The formula for vesting any property in the Sangha stressed the common ownership:

> "Donated to present and future Sangha" (*āgatānāgatasanghassa dinnaṃ.* Literally, the Sangha that came and did not come.)

Because of this very reason, the Sangha has been rated as "an incomparable field for the acquisition of merit" (*anuttaraṃ puññakkhettaṃ)*, and what is donated to the Sangha was declared to bring about the highest fruit in terms of merit (*etesu dinnāni mahapphalāni*).

At the early stages, the Sangha subsisted on food obtained by begging from door to door, wore garments made of rags picked up from the dust-heap or the cemetery, lived under trees or in caves, in forest groves or public buildings and used elementary nature cures in times of ill-health. But as time went on, the Buddha relaxed such rules and paved the way for the Sangha to evolve as a viable institution of proven stability. Buildings and properties were accepted. He enjoined generous donors to "Establish beautiful monasteries" (*vihāre kāraye ramme* — *Cullavagga*, VI, 1, 5: Guruge, 1999, p.196).

Monastics were permitted to accept robes and other requisites. The Buddha himself accepted invitations for lunch and the restriction to begging was gradually relaxed. So were rules pertaining to medicine. In due course, monastics were allowed clarified butter, honey, and molasses as medicine. The Buddha's own cousin was unhappy that the rules for the Sangha were not stringent enough. He wanted monastics to live under trees, wear rags from the dust-heap, eat only what was begged, be vegetarians, and so forth. In his wisdom, the Buddha saw that the Sangha would last as a vibrant institution only if it was flexible. So such strict conduct was allowed for zealous monastics to be adopted voluntarily. The Sangha could thus develop as a human institution responding to needs and challenges of time.

This viability of the Sangha was substantially enhanced by the democratic principles on which its administration and disciplinary control were founded. The Buddha believed in a decentralized Sangha. As his death was approaching, concerned disciples asked him whether a successor was envisaged. The Buddha said, "No" and explained that his teachings would be their teacher.

With no centralized control, the Sangha evolved meeting the demands of each location and time. Whatever be the unit — a whole large city or a small village — the monastics living in that unit were autonomous. They met for fortnightly confessional ceremonies, where the Pātimokkha or Prātimokṣa rules [7] were recited. They made decisions collectively. The question to be decided upon was presented by the most eloquent speaker in the assembly — not by the most senior or most influential. The reason for this stipulation was that the question was clearly presented and the assembly knew the issues to be considered. The question was posed not just once but three times. After each presentation, a vote was taken. The idea was that each vote would enable voters to rethink and re-evaluate. It was hoped that a consensus would develop in the process. If at the third "reading" the vote was not unanimous, the matter was referred to a committee for arbitration. The committee's task was to reformulate the question in a way that points of disagreement were removed as far as possible. It is after such an effort that a matter would be decided by majority vote as a last resort. To this day, this devotion to democratic decision making persists as the most important factor contributing to the lasting effectiveness of the Sangha.

The Buddha also laid down rules for the Sangha to become cohesive and durable. The recruitment of new monastics requires a minimum quorum. Without such a quorum no ordination would be valid. During the long history of Buddhism, countries had to face the problem of having no quorum. When it happened in one coun-

---

[7] These are basic rules of discipline which number 227 in Southern Buddhism and 250-253 in Northern and Vajrayāna Buddhism. The bhikkhunis have around 300 such rules.

try, the number of monastics to restore the Sangha was obtained from another country. For example, when China had no quorum to ordain nuns, Devasārā from Sri Lanka was invited with a team of Sinhala nuns to restore the Bhikkuṇī Order in China. Sri Lanka's Sangha was restored by monks from Thailand in 1753. Despite the differences in Buddhist traditions, the authenticity of the Sangha has been retained to a degree that no other human institution had succeeded.

The Buddha was as pragmatic in the regulation of the Sangha as he was in his doctrines. It is known that he allowed the Sangha to relax some of the minor rules. Ānanda was blamed for not finding out exactly what such minor rules were. It is, however, apparent that some of the variations one might see in the Sangha of differrent traditions could be due to the relaxation of some minor regulations. These really did not affect the integrity of the Sangha: e.g. tailored garments instead of robes and an evening meal (which, quite interestingly, is called medicine). These again are factors which enabled the Sangha to perpetuate itself in countries of climatic conditions different from those of Northern India.

Thus has the Buddhist Sangha remained, without a break, the longest standing monastic system in the world. Its self-renewing and self-regulating capacity has made it a remarkable force which has withstood innumerable obstacles. The confidence which Master Hsing Yun places in the Sangha is more than justified.

The Capacity of the Sangha to Perform a Continually Diversifying Mission

By the time the Buddhist Sangha assumed its final form, it was an organization of monks and nuns, dedicated to a variety of services. It is true that the main purpose of joining the Sangha was to seek one's own liberation through enlightenment. It was the primary concern of monks and nuns. But that goal did not preclude them from making a direct contribution to social well-being.

During the Buddha's life-time itself, the Sangha had differentiated roles. We hear of meditating monastics who concentrated on Insight Meditation. (*Vipassanādhura* or *Vidarśanādhura* — i.e.

vocation of Insight). They engaged themselves in mental cultivation and lived for the most part isolated from society. Whether they continued to do so after their enlightenment is, however, not known. It is most likely they took up services for the welfare of others after reaching Arahanthood. Arahants are shown in Pali Canon and Chinese Āgama Sūtras as engaged in educational and literary activities.

As a distinct group are mentioned monastics who took to educational and literary pursuits. They were said to follow the vocation of books (*ganthadhura*). Their contribution was substantial. They taught both monastics and laity. The Pali Canon and Āgama Sūtras contain discourses given by monks such as Sāriputta, Kaccāyana and Ānanda and literary compositions of both monks and nuns. Especially during the rainy season of four months when monastics stayed in a monastery continuously, they undertook in-depth study of the Buddha's teachings from two points of view:

> *First*, they sought to explain the statements of the Buddha and, with that, began the commentarial literature whose earliest specimens are to be found in the Tipiṭaka itself (i.e. *Culla–* and *Mahā-niddesas*).
>
> *Second*, they pursued scholastic analysis, classification, synthesis, and interpretation of the Buddha's teachings.

It is this process which resulted in the development of the Abhidhamma. In the Northern Buddhist tradition, Śāriputra, the first of the Buddha's two Chief Disciples, is associated with the growth of Abhidharma. (Thich Huyen-Vi, 1971, pp. 381-398)

We also know that monastics specialized in specific areas. A dispute is said to have taken place among specialists of the Dharma, meaning the doctrinal aspects of the Buddha's teachings, (i.e. *Dhammadharas*) and the specialists on rules of discipline and procedures of jurisprudence (i.e. the *Vinayadharas*). An analysis of a work like *Paṭisambhidā magga*, included in the *Khuddakanikāya* of the *Suttapiṭaka*, illustrates the depth of analysis and interpretation which scholar-monastics had achieved. Later, we hear of specialists on specific texts of the Canon: e.g. *Dīghabhāṇakas* (reciters of long discourses), *Majjhimabhāṇakas* (reciters of middle-length discourses), etc.

The tradition of scholastic analysis and interpretation continued after the Buddha and the work of scholar-monastics received approval and recognition. In the third century BCE — over two hundred years after the death of the Buddha — Moggaliputta Tissa, the President of the Third Buddhist Council under the auspices of Emperor Asoka, produced a scholarly work on points of debate and controversy. This book called *Kathāvatthu* (Points of Controversy) is included in the *Abhidhammapiṭaka* and recognized as an integral part of the Canon (Guruge, 1993, pp. 153-154). Myanmar, for example, recognizes three more books of later origin as canonical: *Miḷindapañha*, *Nettippakaraṇa* and *Peṭakopadesa* — all important works of scholarship.

The practice continued in Early Buddhism and has been perpetuated in Southern Buddhism. The Buddhist monastery to this day is a center of learning, where monastics and the lay are educated. The curriculum for the laity had included literacy training and secular knowledge. Indigenous medicine (*Āyurveda*) and astrology (*Jyotiṣa*) have been two vocations for which the basic education was given to the laity by the monastery. Equally significant was the study of languages and literature. Pali, Prakrits, and Sanskrit, including in the last case an enormous body of literature and scientific information, have been preserved as a result of the educational initiatives and efforts of monastics.

As far as the lay society was concerned, the Sangha from its very inception established a symbiotic relationship. The laity maintained the Sangha providing them with the four requisites of food, clothing, shelter and medicine (referred to in Pali Canon as *Catupaccaya* — fourfold requisites). The Sangha reciprocated by serving the laity as teachers and counselors. In the *Sigālovādasutta* of *Dīghanikaya* (D. 31), the reciprocal duties and obligations between the religious or spiritual teacher and a lay devotee are elaborated as follows:

The religious or spiritual teacher —

1. restrains the lay devotees from evil;

2. establishes them in good;
3. teaches them what has not been heard before (= new knowledge);
4. elucidates what has been heard before (= clarifies and reinforces existing knowledge);
5. shows them the way to heaven.[8]

The lay devotee —

(1) extends friendliness to the spiritual teachers in deed,
(2) word, and
(3) thought;
(4) keeps the door open for them for unhindered entrance;
(5) supplies their material needs and creature comforts.

It is to this fruitful relationship that the Buddha referred to in the following verse:

The lay and the homeless alike
Each supporting the other
Accomplish the true doctrine
The peerless refuge from Bondage.

(*Itivuttaka* 107)

This reciprocity between the Sangha and the laity has been so ingrained in early Buddhist societies and so maintained in Southern Buddhism that the Sangha divided itself into two main branches:

(i) forest-dwellers (*vanavāsī* or *araṇyavāsī)* and
(ii) village-dwellers (*gāmavāsī*).

The forest-dwelling monastics lived in hermitages — like monasteries away from the "madding crowd" and spent their time engaged in meditation in perfect isolation. The village-dwelling monastics

---

[8] The deliberate choice of *sagga*, meaning any one of heavenly states, rather than *mokkha, vimutti, nibbāṇa*, meaning liberation, is significant. The laity were not taught for liberation but only for a happier rebirth. Cf. Anāthapiṇḍika episode. Equally important is the assumption here that all religious or spiritual teachers, irrespective of sectarian differences, could lead the laity to heaven or happiness in the next life.

lived in the midst of lay settlements, interacting with people, preaching to them the Dharma, teaching their children, running schools where needed and possible, writing and publishing books, spearheading public and social services and providing leadership to the population.

The Buddhist societies of South and Southeast Asia have viable forest hermitages as well as large numbers of monastics performing services to the laity in cities, towns and rural areas. These same societies developed the tradition of lay Buddhist scholars. Emperor Asoka (circa 299-228 BCE) was perhaps the earliest to prepare and propagate his own anthology of essential Buddhist texts (Cf. Babhru or Bairat Inscription) and interpret a universally valid code of ethics for his subjects (Guruge, 1993, 550-551). Sri Lankan history records instances where lay scholars adjudicated issues in Buddhism (Guruge, 1989, p. 701) and wrote a number of excellent treatises.[9]

The tradition has continued to this day, and lay Buddhist scholars in Southern Buddhism number several thousands. The impressive rates of literacy and educational participation of these societies (when compared with those of neighboring Hindu and Muslim societies) speak eloquently of the effectiveness of the Sangha as pioneers of education. The universalization of primary education in the last century was possible in Myanmar, Sri Lanka and Thailand because the village temple became a modern primary school, conducted by the Sangha. The Sangha has also been responsible for the steady flow of Buddhist literature in local languages. Today, monastics continue to play a leadership role in educating the people to overcome poverty and oppression, to conserve nature and the environment, and to become effective citizens. Though political activities by monastics is not favored by public opinion, some involvement with politics has been inevitable.

---

[9] Among such lay scholars are King Kassapa V (*Dampiyāaṭuvāgäṭapadaya*), Guruḷugomi (*Dharmapradīpikā* and *Amāvatura*) and Vidyācakravarti (*Butsaraṇa, Dahamsaraṇa and Saññgasaraṇa*).

The history of the Sangha has prepared it to perform not only a diversified mission but also one that continues to evolve and diversify. The reciprocal strengthening of the Sangha and the laity has been a hallmark of Buddhism. Grand Master Hsing Yun, therefore, is convinced that "only through dynamic cooperation between the Sangha and the lay followers, between the scholar and the student, will we ever be able to spread the Dharma to all who have a need of it."

Reviving the Buddhist Sangha and Restoring Lost Elements

Grand Master Hsing Yun highlights the joint role to be played by the Sangha and the laity (especially scholars from both groups) for Humanistic Buddhism to usher in social well-being. He has actively undertaken for well-nigh four decades measures to equip the Sangha to become an effective partner. He began by addressing issues specific to Chinese and East Asian Mahāyāna Sangha through periodicals, books, classes and public speeches. Without restricting himself to advocacy, however effective it was, he translated into action his lofty ideas of how the Sangha should be trained to become active promoters of service to people. The Fo Guang Shan Buddhist Order embodies his ideals in practice.

To supplement what he taught, he sent promising monks and nuns to universities in Japan and the USA to begin with, and eventually all over the world. Today, the monastics of the Fo Guang Shan Buddhist Order represent the whole spectrum of Buddhist Studies as developed in the world's most renowned centers of excellence. The Grand Master provides them with the opportunity to earn graduate degrees, Masters and Doctorates, from a number of the highly respected universities. With that body of scholars at the core, he established Colleges of Buddhist Studies with wide-ranging curri-cula and obtained the services of competent scholars of all tradi-tions of Buddhism — from China, Japan, Sri Lanka, Tibet and else-where.

That was not all that Grand Master Hsing Yun has done to revive the Sangha to uphold the ideals of scholarship which have been motivating it from the days of the Buddha. He looked beyond

East Asia to the traditionally Buddhist countries of the rest of the continent. He inspired their monastics to cooperate with him and emulate his example. In one particular initiative, his courageous intervention has proved to be most far-reaching.

Centuries ago, Southern Buddhism lost the *Bhikkhuṇī-sāsana*, the Order of Nuns. It happened before Sri Lanka spread its reformed, unified form of Buddhism to Myanmar, Thailand, Cambodia and Laos. Thus this so-called Theravāda[10] Buddhist world has been deprived of the services of bhikkhuṇis. It is true that women have always been active in the promotion of Buddhism. Many women dedicated themselves to the Buddhist cause by renouncing household life. But the most that they could do was to become observers of ten precepts.[11] Called "*Dasasīlamātās*" (mothers observing the ten precepts), they could not be given higher ordination or *upasampadā*.

The bhikkhus had a valid reason for depriving them of the formal status of bhikkhuṇis. According to the Vīnaya rules, a quorum of both bhikkhus and bhikkhuṇis (ten of each) is absolutely necessary to ordain a bhikkhuṇi. In fact, it was the reason why Sri Lankan nuns had to go to China in two voyages in the fourth century CE. Grand Master Hsing Yun's cooperation with the forward-looking monks of Sri Lanka, in spite of the formidable opposition from certain quarters, resulted in the higher ordination of a number of bhikkhuṇis from Sri Lanka. The historic ceremony took place in February 1998 at Buddha Gaya, the holy spot where Śākyamuni Buddha attained enlightenment. The Fo Guang Shan nuns who participated to form the quorum of bhikkhuṇis traced their continuous lineage from the restoration of *Upasampadā* in China by the Sri Lankan Bhikkhuṇī Devasārā and her colleagues.

---

[10] As regards the inapplicability of the term Theravāda as a description of Southern Buddhism today, see Guruge, 2000 pp. 88-92 and 111-118 and *The Buddhist* (YMBA, Colombo), Vesak Number 2000.

[11] This is a state more or less equivalent to that of a novice. The ten precepts are to abstain from (1) killing (2) stealing (3) sexual activity (4) falsehood (5) stupefying liquor and drugs (6) eating at inappropriate hours (7) adorning oneself and using cosmetics (8) dancing, singing and comic shows (9) using large seats and beds, and (10) handling gold and silver.

By this most timely step, Grand Master Hsing Yun strengthened the Sangha of Southern Buddhism. Now the Sangha of Sri Lanka, Myanmar, Thailand, Cambodia, Laos, India, Bangladesh, Nepal and elsewhere can give women an equal chance to play their rightful role in spiritual life. He also accomplished an historically significant *rapprochement* between Northern and Southern Buddhism in a crucial ecclesiastical act (*Vinayakamma*). The ecumenical significance of this joint action may take more time to be widely recognized. But its impact of bringing the Buddhists of the world together for the promotion of a humanistic approach to spiritual life is unequivocal. Equally important is that the Grand Master's revival of *Bhikkhuṇi-sāsana* in Sri Lanka is tantamount to repaying a debt which East Asia owed this predominantly Buddhist nation.

Grand Master Hsing Yun has thus concentrated on restoring to the Sangha the historic status it enjoyed in Early Buddhism. It stems from his conviction that a competent, well-educated, resourceful and efficient Sangha is absolutely necessary to bring Buddhism to the doorstep of every man, woman and child of the world.

Role of Scholars and Intellectual Advancement

In Grand Master Hsing Yun's vision, an equally important role in the propagation of Humanistic Buddhism has to be played by the scholar, whether he or she is a monastic or a lay person. The Buddha encouraged intellectual pursuit by his reliance on the critical acumen of the human being. He placed his doctrine for acceptance only after investigation. "Come and see for yourself" (*Ehipassika*) was his clarion call. He disapproved of blind faith. His Dhamma is "to be known by the wise by oneself" (*paccattam veditabbo viññūhi*). Once Sāriputta, his first disciple, praised him as the greatest Buddha. "Do you know the Buddhas of the past? Do you know the Buddhas of the future?" the Buddha asked him. Sāriputta had to admit that he did not know any of them. "How can you then call me the greatest of the Buddhas?" was the Buddha's response (D. 16). Thus was stressed the basic element of the scientific method by which all scholarship is guided: namely, the strictest dependence on reliable evidence for every conclusion.

That the Sangha pursued scholarly research by way of analysis, synthesis, exegesis and interpretation of the Dharma during the life-time of the Buddha, and most certainly under his own direction, is borne out by some elements of the Canon of Early Buddhism. The discourses were grouped together on two distinct criteria:

(i) According to literary form: the *navangabuddhasāsana* (ninefold teachings of the Buddha): namely, *sutta* (discourses), *geyya* (chants), *veyyākaraṇa* (analyses), *gāthā* (stanzas), *udāna* (inspirational utterances), *ituvuttaka* (thus it was said) *jātaka* (birth stories), *abbutadhamma* (supernormal or paranormal) and *vedalla* (question and answer).

(ii) According to length and content as *Nikāyas* or *Āgamas* [12]: namely, *Dīghanikāya* and *Majjhimanikāya* (Long- and Middle-length Discourses), *Saṃyuttanikāya* (Discourses grouped according to subjects, audiences and such other kindred factors); *Anguttaranikāya* (Discourses grouped according to the number of elements covered); and *Khuddakanikāya* (Minor Texts, mainly poetical compositions and short texts).

Dhammapada, whose popularity is evinced by its many versions from ancient times and by its ever increasing translations into modern languages, shows the excellent result of compiling a collection of inspirational utterances of the Buddha. *Suttanipāta* is a well-conceived anthology of beautiful poetical compositions. So are *Theragāthā* and *Therīgāthā* where lyrical outpourings of emotions of monks and nuns, motivated by spiritual attainments, are presented.

Another piece of evidence about Buddhist scholarship of the Buddha's lifetime are the indexes and abstracts prepared especially for the Vinaya rules of discipline. When Jina Mahāvīra, the founder of Jainism, passed away a few years before the Buddha, Jainas began to quarrel among themselves on the authenticity of each

---

[12] In the Canon of the Sarvāstivādins in Sanskrit, the divisions are named *Dīrghāgama*, *Madhyamāgama*, *Saṃyuktāgama*, *Ekottarāgama* and *Kṣudrakāgama*.

one's interpretation of Jaina teachings. Sāriputta, as mentioned earlier, initiated a project to prevent similar things happening to the Buddha's teachings. The product of this project as recorded in the *Saṅgīti-* and *Dasuttarasuttas* of the Dīghanikāya continues to baffle scholars. What he had done is to prepare a comprehensive, well-organized list of keywords under which the entire body of the Buddha's teachings can be subsumed and systematically arranged for ready recall. The exhaustive indexing of the details of the Buddha's teachings in these suttas testify to the methodological skills of Śāriputra as well as his astonishing understanding of the need for facilitating retrieval of information. That he was an intellectual and contributed to the systematization of the Buddha's teachings is amply illustrated.

As noted earlier, Sāriputta is also credited with the scholastic undertaking which resulted in the Abhidhammapiṭaka. The kind of detailed analysis to which the teachings of the Buddha were subjected, especially with regard to psychology and matter, paved the way for the continuing tradition of study and research, explanation and interpretation. New works were accepted on merit into the Canon.

It is this devotion to scholarship which enabled Buddhist scholars to make a significant contribution to the elaboration of Buddha's teachings. In Early Buddhism the emphasis has been on commentaries, subcommentaries, glossaries and such other works which facilitate the understanding of the canonical works. These kinds of exegetical works flourished in Southern Buddhism. Buddhaghosa, Dhammapala, Buddhadatta, Ananda, Culla-Dhammapala, Upasena, Mahānāma, Kassapa, Vajirabuddhi, Khema, and Anuruddha were the most noteworthy figures in this movement. They are credited with translating into Pali the old Sinhala commentaries, which were extant up to about the twelfth century. Equally important in Southern Buddhism are monastic historians who produced historical chronicles of a wide variety and preserved a remarkably accurate history of Buddhism.

The Mahāyāna scholars proceeded in a different way: they produced new treatises with the stress placed on the philosophical and doctrinal analysis and elaboration of basic teachings of the Buddha. Aśvaghoṣa, the pioneering Mahāyāna scholar, was closely associated with the Kushan Emperor, Kaniṣka I, in holding the Fourth Buddhist Council in Jalandhara, Kashmir (circa 1st or 2nd century CE). His works include two beautiful ornate poems, *Buddhacarita* (Life of the Buddha), and *Saundaranandakāvya* (The story of the Buddha's half-brother Nanda whose marriage to Sundari was stopped on account of his being ordained a monk by the Buddha); a play, *Śāriputraprakaraṇa* (on the conversion of Śāriputra) and the inspiring evangelical treatise, *Mahāyāna-śraddhotpāda* (Awakening of Faith in the Mahāyāna). A later exponent of the Vaibhāṣika school, Vasubandhu produced *Abhi-dharmakoṣa* — an exhaustive work whose impact outside India is to be traced to the Kosha or Chü-she and Pi-t-an (< abhidhamma) school of China and the Kusha school of Japan.

Among the best known and most widely influential scholars were Nāgārjuna, Āryadeva, Asanga and his younger brother Vasubandhu. The Mādhyamika school, founded by Nāgārjuna, examined in depth the instrinsic nature or characteristic of things (i.e. *Svabhāva* or own-being) in relation to the twelve factors of Dependent Origination (*Paṭiccasamuppāda*). Nāgārjuna's conclusion was that anything which arises dependent on other things has no *svabhāva* or "own-being" and, therefore, is futile, void, and empty (*śūnya*). Nāgārjuna's and Āryadeva's works on this subject were so influential, that the concept of Śūnyatā pervaded the thinking in Mahāyāna schools throughout the world.

A similar lasting influence has been exerted by Asanga who elaborated on Nāgārjuna's concept of *Svabhāva*, presenting in the process the theory of three marks of experience of reality as *parikalpita* (imagined), *paratantra* (dependent) and *pariniṣpanna* (absolute or perfected). Similarly far-reaching in impact was Asanga's extension of the doctrine of six consciousnesses (i.e. those of the five senses and the mind) in Early Buddhism by adding two more: namely, *Ālayavijñāna* (storehouse-consciousness — the basis for all feelings, thoughts, ideas and where seeds of *karma* accumulated) and *Manas* (what induced one to the wrong belief that *Ālayavijñāna* was eternal and unchanging). He and Vasubandhu founded the Yogācāra or Vijñānavāda school which stressed that all reality existed only in the mind (*cittamātra* = mind only).

These scholarly interpretations of the Buddha's teachings brought into prominence the importance of logic in debate and controversy. Thus Buddhist scholarship promoted, through an on-going confrontation with Hindu logicians, a system of Buddhist logic. Names like Dinnāga, Dharmapāla, Śīlabhadra, Dharmakīrti and Candragomin are recalled with appreciation for their contribution not only to Buddhist logic but also to the evolution of Indian epistemology.

Also to be noted is that several among the above-mentioned scholars were connected with the premier Buddhist University of Nalandā (2nd to 11th century CE). Nāgārjuna, Āryadeva, Dharmapāla, Śīlabhadra and Dharmakīrti were abbots of Nalandā and exerted enormous influence in the spread of Buddhism beyond the frontiers of the Indian Sub-continent. Xuanzang (602-644 CE) studied at Nalandā under the guidance of Śīlabhadra.

Another very important service which scholars rendered to the propagation of Buddhism has been the translation of texts to foreign languages. The history of Buddhism in China is replete with such illustrious names of translators as Dharmarakṣa, Kumārajīva (undoubtedly the greatest of missionary translators), Paramārtha, Guṇavarman, Guṇabhadra and Śāntarakṣita. Their counterparts in Tibetan Buddhism are Padmasambhava and Atiśa Dīpankara.

There is no doubt that Grand Master Hsing Yun's appraisal of the role of the scholar in bringing Buddhism to every being is founded on these historical precedents. His vision of Buddhist scholarship today — particularly with regard to the promotion of Humanistic Buddhism — is threefold:

(i) Establish contacts with scholars specializing in various aspects of Buddhism and promote cooperation and collaboration among them;

(ii) Create university-level centers of excellence where renowned scholars can be engaged in training young scholars through teaching and research; and

(iii) Promote the interaction of scholars in in-depth study of Humanistic Buddhism through international seminars, conferences and research initiatives.

Translating this vision into concrete action, he proceeded on a program of institution building. At the headquarters of the Fo Guang Shan Buddhist Order in Kaohsiung, South Taiwan, was established the Fo Guang Shan College of Humanities and Social Science. In Chia-Yi County in Central Taiwan, Nan Hua University was developed into a full-scale seat of higher learning with all modern facilities. At Ilan in East Taiwan is Fo Guang University, with a significant research and publication program. In Los Angeles County, California, USA, Hsi Lai University offers a wide variety of courses in Religious Studies from BA to Ph.D. and a comprehensive range of courses in Business Administration for BA, MBA, Executive MBA and Post-MBA Certificates, besides custom-made courses in English as a Second Language and Continuing Education.

For enhanced networking among international scholars, the International Academy of Buddhism, attached to Hsi Lai University, and the Fo Guang Shan Cultural and Educational Foundation in Kaohsiung sponsor conferences, research projects and publications. The Hsi Lai University Press, Hacienda Heights, and the International Buddhist Translation Center in San Diego are primary centers for the translation and publication of scholarly and instructional materials.

The first three volumes of the Hsi Lai Journal of Humanistic Buddhism, published by the International Academy of Buddhism, have already been issued with research papers on Humanistic Buddhism. More institutional building in such far-flung places as Australia and South Africa are in the Grand Master's plans.

All these activities discussed in relation to the spreading of the Dharma by marshalling the Sangha and the laity, scholar and student, demonstrate how the cause of Humanistic Buddhism for social well-being is amply served.

Buddhism in the Human Realm

The Buddha, the Man

Grand Master Hsing Yun draws our attention to the importance of Buddhism in the Human Realm when he says,

> "In Buddhism, the human realm is the most important realm of all. The human realm is the realm where great transformations can occur. Not only have all the Buddhas in the universe achieved enlightenment in this realm, but this also is where great sages and great Bodhisattvas appear to preach the Dharma. Bodhidharma, Faxian, Xuangzang and many others underwent great hardships solely for the good of sentient beings living in the human realm."

The Pali Canon contains a few but significant autobiographical references attributed to the Buddha.[13] He spoke of the

---

[13] Bhikkhu Ñāṇamoḷi (1972) has been extensively utilized for canonical references on the life of the Buddha. I have considered his translations as well as those in Pali Text Society publications and made such changes as I found desirable to be closer to the original Pali, for which I depended entirely on PTS editions.

luxury in which he was brought up in his father's home. "I was delicate, most delicate, supremely delicate. Lily ponds were made for me at my father's house solely for my benefit.... I used no sandalwood that was not from Benares. My turban, tunic, lower garments and cloak were all made of Benares cloth. A white parasol was held over me day and night so that no cold or heat or dust or grit or dew might inconvenience me."

He has mentioned that three palaces were constructed for him — one for each season. He has referred to his life style by referring to the way the servants were treated: "Though meals of broken rice with lentil soup are given to servants and retainers in other people's houses, in my father's house white rice and meat were given to them."

He proceeded further, "While I had such power and good fortune... the vanity of youth... the vanity of health... the vanity of life entirely left me." (A III, 38) Elsewhere he referred to his youth again and said,

> "Being subject to birth, aging, ailment, death, sorrow and defilement, I sought after what was also subject to these things."
>
> (M. 26).
>
> "Later, while still young, in the first phase of life, I shaved off my hair and beard — though my mother and father wished otherwise and grieved with tearful faces — and I put on yellow cloth and went forth from house life to homelessness."
>
> (M. 26, 36, 85, 100)

In these same texts the Buddha related his experience with the two teachers, Āḷāra Kālāma and Uddaka Rāmaputta: "I soon learned the teaching. I claimed that as far as lip reciting and rehearsal of [their] teaching went I could speak with knowledge (*ñānavāda*) and assurance (*theravāda*), and that I knew and saw — and there were others who did likewise." (Ibid) [14]

---

[14] Bhikkhu Nānamoli (1972, 13) translates this passage as follows: "I could speak with knowledge (*ñānavada*) and assurance (*theravāda*)" depending on the

The brief account of his life in the forest as an ascetic underlines the fear and dread he felt as any ordinary person: "On such specially holy nights... I dwelt in some awesome abodes as orchard shrines, woodland shrines and tree shrines which make the hair stand up. And while I dwelt there, a deer would approach me or a peacock would knock off a branch or wind would rustle the leaves. Then I thought: Surely this is the fear and dread coming." (M. 4)

He also has described how strenuous practices affected him physically: "I stopped in-breaths and out-breaths in my mouth. When I did so, there was a loud sound of winds coming from my ear-holes. ...I stopped the in-breaths and out-breaths in my mouth, nose and ears. When I did so, violent winds racked my head... there were violent pains in my head... violent winds carved up my belly, and... there was violent burning in my belly." (M. 36, 85, 100)

The same texts attribute to him an account of how the stringent fasting affected his body: "My body reached a state of extreme emaciation; my limbs became like joint segments of vine or bamboo stems, because of eating so little. My back became like a camel's hoof; the projections of my spine stood forth like corded beads; my ribs jutted out as gaunt as crazy rafters of an old roofless barn; the gleam of my eyes sunk far down in their sockets looked like the gleam of water sunk far down in a deep well; my scalp shriveled and withered as a green gourd shrivels and withers in the wind and sun. If I touched my belly skin, I encountered my backbone; if I touched my backbone, I encountered my belly skin, for my belly skin cleaved to my backbone. If I made water or evacuated my bowels, I fell over on my face there. If I tried to ease my body by rubbing my limbs with my hands, the hair, rotted at the

---

Commentary which explains *theravāda* as *thirabhāvavādaṃ* (=statement of stability and hence assurance) and adds "*thero aham attho*" (The meaning is "I am a *thera* or an elder"). As commentators display a tendency to invent etymologies based on the similarity of words, I am inclined to think that the word *Theravāda* existed in the same sense that the Buddhists use: i. e. the doctrine of the elders.

roots, fell away from my body as I rubbed, because of eating so little." (M. 36, 85, 100) [15]

An all too natural inclination to abandon his goal figures in a beautiful poem where the Buddha's sentiments are attributed to Māra the Tempter (Guruge 1993-1, 169):

"O you are thin and pale,
And you are in the Death's presence too.
A thousand parts are pledged to death,
But life still holds one part of you.
Live, sir! Life is the better way;
You can gain merit if you live;
Come live the holy life and pour
Libations on the holy fires,
And thus a world of merit gain.
What can you do by struggling now?
The path of struggling too is rough
And difficult and hard to bear."

(*Suttanipāta*. III, 2)

What came to his mind at this stage is stated as follows: "But by this grueling penance, I have attained no distinction higher than **the human state.** ...Might there be another way to enlightenment?" Here is recalled an incident from his childhood: "I thought of a time when my Śākyan father was working and I was sitting in the cool shade of a rose-apple tree... and entered upon and abode in the First Meditation... Then following that memory there came the recognition that it was the way to enlightenment." (M. 36, 85, 100).

The attainment of enlightenment is further described in his own words. (M. 36, S. XII 65, D. 14). It ends with the explanation: "As long as I did not know by direct knowledge, as it actually is, so long did I make no claim to have discovered the enlightenment. But as soon as I knew by direct knowledge, as it actually is... then I

---

[15] Representations of the Buddha-to-be in penance (called "Fasting Buddha") had been a popular theme in Gandhara sculpture. See Heinrich Zimmer: *The Art of Indian Asia*, Bollingen Foundation, New York 1955 Vol II, Plate 65.

[16] Pali Uttarimanussa means "above or beyond the state of a human" whereas Lokottara signifies "supra-mundane, above or beyond the world."

claimed to have discovered the enlightenment that is supreme in the world with its deities, its Māras and its divinities, in this generation with its monks and Brahmans, with its princes and men." (S. XXII, 26; Mv. 1; S. LVI 11)

It is only here that the Buddha is shown as making a reference to Māras, divinities and such other supernatural beings. But they are mentioned along with monks and Brahmans and princes and men to describe the world or rather the universe in which enlightenment was supreme.

Two more autobiographical statements occur in the *Mahāparinibbāṇasutta*. (D. 16) One is on his renunciation and mission:

"But twenty-nine I was when I renounced
The world, Subhadda, seeking after Good.
For fifty years and one year more, Subhadda,
Since I went out, a pilgrim have I been
Through the wide realm of System and of Dhamma—
Outside of that no victory can be won."

The other is a touching tone on his imminent death: "I, too, O Ananda, am now grown old and full of years, my journey is drawing to its close, I have reached my sum of days, I am turning eighty years of age; just as a worn-out cart, Ananda, can be kept going only with thongs, so, methinks, the body of the Buddha can only be kept going by bandaging it."

Equally moving is the statement in agreement with Ānanda: "So it is, Ānanda, so it is. Youth has to age, health has to sicken, life has to die. All my limbs are flaccid and wrinkled, my body is bent forward, and there seems a change in the sense faculties of my eyes, ears, nose, tongue and bodily sensations.

Shame on you, sordid Age,
Maker of Ugliness.
Age has now trampled down
The form that once had grace.
To live a hundred years
Is not to cheat Decay,
That gives quarter to none

And tramples down all things."

(S. XLVIII, 41)

Ānanda once observed, "He was injured when a splintered rock hit his foot." (S. IV, 13) When Vakkali in an exceedingly poor state of health excused himself for not visiting the Buddha, the Buddha's reply was "Enough, Vakkali, why do you want to see my filthy body (*pūtikāya*)?" (S. XXII, 87) What is significant in all these autobiographical statements is that the Buddha appears, speaks and acts as a human being — a mortal with emotions of fear and anxiety, and subject to human conditions. He was subject to illness and old age. (D. 16; S. XLVII,9) He expected to be so weak in his old age that he would have to be carried about in a gurney. (M. 104)

In the earliest texts of the Pali Canon, this was how the Buddha was viewed by his disciples. He was a person of human dimensions: only four finger-breadths taller than his half-brother, Nanda. (Sv. Pac. 92). Both Nanda and Mahākassapa are believed to have resembled the Buddha and sometimes confused disciples who mistook them for the Buddha. In the same Vinaya text, the dimensions of the Buddha's robe is given as nine spans by six spans (approximately 9 feet by 6 feet, according to Welivitiye Sorata: Sri Sumangala Sinhala Dictionary sv. *viyata*). And the Buddha and Mahakassapa are said to have exchanged their robes.

The charisma of the Buddha induced people to ask who he really was. *Anguttaranikāya* records a conversation with Brahman Doṇa:

Sir, will you be a god (*deva*)?
No, Brahman.
Will you be a heavenly angel (*gandhabba*)?
No, Brahman.
Will you be a spirit (*yakkha*)?
No, Brahman.
Will you be a human being (*manussa*)?
No, Brahman.
Then, Sir, What indeed will you be?

> Brahman, the taints by which I might be a deva, gandhabba, yakkha or manussa have been all abandoned in me, cut off at the root, made like a palm stump, done away with, and are no more subject to arising in the future. Just as a blue or red or white lotus is born in water, grows in water and stands up above the water untouched by it, so too I, who was born in this world and grew in the world, have transcended the world, and I live untouched by the world. Remember me as one who is enlightened. (*Buddho'ti maṃ Brāhmaṇa dhārehi*)
>
> (A. IV, 36).

The reason advanced for not being any one other than a Buddha is purely ethical. This as well as numerous other references in the Pali Canon would show that, during the lifetime of the Buddha itself, **Buddhahood** had become a distinct state, *above* and *different* from that of a human being.

In spite of the increasing tendency to elevate the Buddha to the level of a Great or Super Man (*Mahāpurisa*, Sanskrit *Mahāpuruṣa*) with thirty-two major and eighty minor characteristics (*lakkhaṇa* or *lakṣaṇa*), and the later introduction of such concepts as *Dhyānibuddhas*, the three *Kāyas* or bodies of the Buddha, a Primeval or Cosmic Buddha (*ādibuddha*), and Buddhas in innumerable Buddha worlds, the overriding belief among Buddhists of all traditions is that Buddhahood is to be attained in the Human Realm, as Grand Master Hsing Yun has stated emphatically.

In fact, the same belief exists with regard to advanced spiritual attainments. This is how Lewis Lancaster explains it:

> The rebirth process is determined by karma, the actions and the results of those actions. When we define karma, it has three ways of being created. These three are through the activities of the body, speech, and thought. Once again we see the central position of a human in the three actions involving the body, sense organs, and mental processes. The non-human births also have karma but it is often

> instinctive or inevitable. Animals have little control over the acting out of that state of existence, they are controlled by a karmic effect. Even the deities seem to have little control over events, they live out their ordained life until the karma that creates the divine state is exhausted. Some deities can only stay in the upper state until they have a thought and the moment a thought occurs, they are reborn immediately in another destiny. Other deities have warning signs of the end of their stay in one of the heavens; the flower garlands around their bodies begin to wilt. Suddenly like a candle that is blown out, they revert to another rebirth. While we must experience the fruit of our karma in this human existence, there is the potential for achieving enlightenment, something seldom available, even to the deities in the heavens.
>
> (Lancaster 2000 p. 123)

A Process of Perfection of Human Personality

Almost all Suttas of the Pali Canon and Āgama Sūtras were preached by the Buddha to human beings. His Path of Deliverance or, more precisely, the "Path leading to the end of suffering," is to be pursued by human beings. A human being becomes an Arahant or a Buddha. The incomparable perfect enlightenment is to be attained by a human being only.

There is a number of discourses, including the *Abhidhamma*, which are said to be addressed to gods and non-human beings. The tradition about the doctrines of *Abhidhamma* is that the Buddha preached it in Tusita heaven to a deity who was Queen Mahamāyā in her previous life. There appears to be a common characteristic of sermons or texts described as preached to gods or deities. These are either poetical compositions as the Mahāmangalasutta (Suttanipāta II, 4) or products of scholastic analysis, synthesis and interpretation like the *Abhidhamma*. In a similar manner Mahāyānasūtras are addressed to large numbers of Bodhisattvas, Mahāsattvas, deities and other supernormal beings as interlocutors. For example, the Lankāvatārasūtra in a later preamble has Rāvaṇa, the mythical demonic king of Lanka, as the interlocutor. *Mahāyānādhisamayasūtra* has his equally mythical brother, Vibhīṣaṇa. In other discourses in the Pali Canon and Āgama Sūtras, the audience as well as interlocutors are human beings, though later preambles or epilogues depict gods and deities as invisible listeners: e.g. *Dhammacakkappavattanasutta* (S. V, LVI, II) and *Mahāsamayasutta* (D. 20).

It has been the universal view of Buddhism that a person has the opportunity to better himself or herself ethically and spiritually only in the human sphere (S. XV). In the words of Grand Master Hsing Yun, "the human realm is the realm where great transformations can occur." As we have already noted, sentient beings exist at so many different levels. The denizens of hells, hungry ghosts (*peta* or *preta*, literally departed ones), Titans or demons (*asuras*) or animals (*tiracchīna* or *tiraścīna*) are said to be incapable of being guided toward self-perfection on account of their miserable conditions. We know for certain that it is true at least with regard to animals. The divine beings in the six sensual spheres, on the contrary, are too engrossed in the enjoyment of sensual pleasures and are, therefore, too distracted to take an interest in the Dharma. The long-living beings of the fine-material (*rūpāvacara*) Brahma-worlds and of the immaterial (*arūpāvacara*) Brahma-worlds are also conceived to be beyond self-improvement. The human being has a short enough span of life to be conscious of suffering and death, an intelligence to grasp the meaning of life and concepts of good and evil, and, thus, a desire for and a capacity of self-improvement, self-perfection, and liberation.

In *Suhṛdlekhā*, attributed to Nāgārjuna, this concept is elaborated as follows:

> Since to attain human existence after existence as an animal
> Is more difficult than for a turtle to put its neck
> Into a hole of a yoke tossed about in an ocean,
> Make life fruitful, Oh King, by acting properly.

To entertain an erroneous view, to be born among
The animals, spirits, and denizens of hell,
To be born a savage in a far-off place where there is no Dharma,
To be born a dumb person or a long-living god—

Any one of these births is unsatisfactory.
These therefore comprise the eight obstacles.
After having encountered a satisfactory juncture free of them,
Endeavor to avert the possibility of (re)birth.

(Leslie Kawamura [Tr.], 1975, verses 59-64)

The unique opportunity, which only a human being has to attain the highest of spiritual attainments in one's own life-time, has been underscored by all traditions of Buddhism. To be born a human being is very difficult, the Buddha said in the Dhammapada (*Kiccho manussapaṭilābho* — Dp. 182). The saying *Dullabhaṃ ca manussattaṃ,* meaning that the state of a human being is rare, is quoted more often, even though a canonical reference to it cannot be found. (See also M. 129)

It is true that the Buddha decried the human body as a putrid mass of rotting substances to which one could not be attached. The decaying body is a subject of meditation that was recommended as the first of the Four Foundations of Mindfulness (D. 22, M. — *Satipaṭṭhānasutta*). The impermanence of the body could be most dramatically demonstrated through anatomical and physiological changes of decay, sickness, death and the decomposition of the cadaver. Those who reveled in life with such total abandon as to forget the realities of existence needed to be reminded. The Buddha did so by drawing attention to the futility of being overly attached to the body and bodily pleasures. Addressed to lustfully inclined persons in particular, the efficacy of this approach is based on the element of shock. But unlike some ascetics of the time, the Buddha neither advocated nor tolerated the neglect and torment of the human body. He recognized the paramount importance of the human body as the means through which one improved oneself spiritually and reached ultimate enlightenment.

He was conscious of the need for nourishment and good health. That was the foundation of the Middle Path of avoiding self-mortification as much as self-indulgence. He considered hunger to be the worst ailment (*jigucchā paramā rogā* — Dp. 204) and good health to be the highest advantage (*ārogyā paramā lābhā* — Dp. 203). The first catechism a novice monastic learns is that all beings subsist on food (*sabbe sattā āhāraṭṭhitikā*). The rules of the Vinaya show that the Buddha wanted his disciples to be conscious of cleanliness, personal hygiene and good appearance. Hair and beard were shaven mainly for health and hygienic reasons. The monastics were required to be of such good appearance and behavior as to convert the non-believers and increase the good dispositions which the converted had for them. It is remarkable that the influence of the monastic standards had such an overall effect on society. Buddhist societies are known to maintain high standards of personal hygiene and environmental sanitation even under precarious economic conditions.

The human realm, according to the Buddhist view, has another significance. It is a state in which a being has pleasurable and hence desirable experiences. In an oft-repeated benediction are listed the following: *āyu* (longevity), *vaṇṇa* (good complexion), *sukham* (comfort or good health) and *balam* (strength or power). The alternation of the favorable and the unfavorable is emphasized in the teaching on the eightfold worldly conditions (*aṭṭhaloka-dhamma*): profit and loss (*lābho alābho*), fame and infamy (*yaso ayaso*), blame or insult and praise (*nindā pasaṃsā*), happiness and misery (*sukha dukkha*). Among worldly gains of being a person of compassion are listed such mundane joys as being able to sleep soundly, getting up soundly, not being disturbed by nightmares, being liked by humans and gods, not being hurt by fire, poison or weapons, having a clear facial complexion and dying without losing consciousness (*Anguttaranikāya* V, 342).

The Buddha's ideal of a perfect person is laconically presented in *Karaṇīyamettasutta* (*Suttanipāta* I, 8). He or she had to be clever or smart in achieving the objective of attaining the ultimate tranquillity (*atthakusala* or *arthakuśala*). The qualities of such a person are listed as follows:

- Efficient and effective (*sakko*)
- Honest or straight (*ujū*)
- Perfectly straightforward (*sūjū*)
- Amenable (*suvaco*)
- Soft or gentle (*mudu*)
- Not excessively proud (*anatimānī*)
- Contented (*santussako*)
- Easily maintained — i.e. an easy guest (*subharo*)
- With little to do — i.e. not a busy body (*appakicco*)
- Of simple life (*sallahukavutti*)
- Restraint in senses (*santindriyo*)
- Mature (*nipako*)
- Not deceitful (*appagabbho*)
- Not overly attached to households (*ananugiddho*)
- Not committing even the smallest fault which the wise may blame in others (*na ca khuddam samācare kiñci yena viññu pare upavadeyyum*).

Such a person's thinking is saturated with the fervent wish that all beings be well, safe and with happy minds.

The acquisition of these qualities for being a perfect human being of compassion and loving kindness or for becoming proficient in accomplishing the objective of liberation in the peaceful bliss (*santaṃ padam*) of Nibbāṇa is a process to be set in motion and completed in this life in the human realm. The Buddha's teachings, therefore, place as much importance on **the life here** as on **life hereafter**, which includes ultimate liberation. "One rejoices here and having passed away one rejoices. The doer of good rejoices in both (*Idha nandati pecca nandati — puññakārī ubhayattha nandati*) is the reward that one gets for being good," says a Dhammapada verse (Dp. 18). The opposite is also said about doers of bad deeds: "One repents or regrets here. One regrets that one had done evil.

Having passed away one regrets. The evil-doer repents or regrets in both" (Dp. 17). *Iha* (here), *param* (hereafter) and *ubhayattha* (in both) are terms which have pervaded the entire ethical system of the Buddha.

How this concept promoted a humanistic approach to social well-being is illustrated by the programs of public service, on the one hand, and intensive campaigns for ethical and spiritual awakening of the people, on the other, of Emperor Asoka. In Rock Edict VI, he explained his motivation:

> "The welfare of the whole world is considered by me my duty... There is no higher work than the welfare of the whole world. Whatever effort I make to discharge my debt to living beings, I will cause them to be happy **here** and they will also attain heaven **hereafter**. (*idha* and *paratrā svagam*)"

Again in Rock Edict XI, he said,

> "There is no such gift as the gift of Dharma, proclamation of Dharma, sharing of Dharma and association with Dharma... This is good. This should be done. Doing so one attains happiness in **this world** and **hereafter** (*iloka* and *parata*)"

In Rock Edict XV, Emperor Asoka admonished the senior official of state,

> "You are indeed able to inspire confidence for their **welfare and happiness in this world** and **the next** (*hidalogika-pālalokikāye*)"
>
> (Guruge 1993 pp. 560, 566, 571)

So has the tradition continued.

Humanistic Buddhism, as interpreted by Grand Master Hsing Yun, reiterates with redoubled emphasis that the teachings of the Buddha are for the human realm and they present a process of perfection of human personality for the well-being of people here in this world as well as hereafter.

Wisdom and Compassion

Buddhism: Passive or Active?

In an outspoken assessment of Buddhism in practice, Grand Master Hsing Yun says,

> "It is a real pity that so many Buddhists, especially when they first begin to practice, place so much emphasis on long retreats and on liberating themselves from the cycle of birth and death. These are important concerns, but remember, no one is going to achieve liberation from the cycle of birth and death if he has not figured out how to live as a human being in the human realm.
>
> All of us must live fully, virtuously and compassionately in this world before we can ever expect to transcend anything. In the past, Buddhism too often was characterized by passivity and inactivity. Buddhists too often were content to 'follow conditions' and not create them themselves. Without a vision of our future, Buddhism will continue to languish in its cocoon, and by doing that, funda-

> mentally contradict some of its most basic principles."

Never before in the history of Buddhism has this reminder been more relevant and urgent as now. The teachings of the Buddha are being sought by an increasing clientele throughout the world. Each has a different need.

It is with hope and faith that one looks to Buddhism to fulfill it. One may come from a totally different religious and cultural background as a new-comer to Buddhism. Another could be a born Buddhist who, after years of either complete disinterest or perfunctory observation of ritual, returns to his or her faith with renewed interest. Both of them could have a multiplicity of objectives: some may be seeking serenity and peace of mind in a life full of cares and socio-economic pressure; others may look for solutions to serious psycho-somatic problems such as anger and paranoia, depression and hyperactivity or an inexplicable lack of interest in life. Between them there could be others whose expectations from Buddhism could be spiritual, intellectual, social or emotional. It is significant that Buddhism has evolved into a religious tradition which can effectively serve all of them.

The principal advantage which Buddhism has is the unfailing inspiration derivable from the life and words of Śākyamuni Buddha. In his mission, he served such a wide variety of people. He went to them or they came to him. It is true that his main objective was to guide as many as he could to the goal of ending suffering. He himself spent six years of isolation and penance with this end in view. But from the moment he had reached his goal, he was no longer a passive enjoyer of the spiritual bliss he had achieved. He stepped into the world as an active worker for other's well-being and happiness. Both by precept and example, he encouraged every disciple to be a preacher, educator and an effective activist. Early Buddhism records incidents in which the Buddha and his immediate disciples were actively engaged in solving others' problems.

Well known are stories of Angulimāla and Ālavaka. The former was a bandit who had already murdered nine hundred and ninety-nine people, and his mother was about to be the thousandth victim. The other was reportedly a cannibal who had terrorized people into bringing him a baby each day. The Buddha met them both at grave personal risk to himself and converted them to a life of virtue. When Kisā Gotamī came to the Buddha with her dead son in her arms, he sent her on a mission to find a mustard seed from a house that had not seen death; of course, at the end of the day's search, she was ready, as intended by the Buddha, to accept death as an inevitable fact of life. The Buddha was there to open the eyes of a grieving king that a daughter's birth was as much an occasion for celebration as that of a son or even better.

He rushed to the aid of a neglected sick monk on whom he attended and declared to monastics, "Those who wait on the sick do really attend on me." So concerned was the Buddha on human suffering that he would not preach to a tired and hungry man until he had his meal. To an old father, neglected by his children, he composed a set of verses praising his cane as his only support; the verses had to be sung only once in public before the errant sons resumed their responsibility. The vast narrative literature of Early Buddhism is full of hundreds of incidents when the Buddha and his disciples went beyond their missionary functions of preaching and educating people and stepped in to help solve their problems. The Buddha has upheld the importance of such public services as water supplies, parks, roads and bridges as acts of merit.

The tradition continued as we see once again from multiple social welfare activities of Emperor Asoka. Rock Edit II says,

(a) King Devānampriya Priyadarśi (i.e. Asoka) installed two kinds of medical treatment: medical treatment for humans and medical treatment for animals

(b) Medicinal herbs, beneficial to humans and beneficial to beast, were brought and planted wherever they were not found;

(c) Wherever they did not exist, roots and fruit were brought and planted ; and

(d) Along roads, wells were dug and trees planted for the use of animals and men.

Piller Edict VII continues to list further welfare measures:

- On roads, too, banyan trees were caused to be planted so that they would provide shade for beast and man;
- Mango groves were caused to be planted;
- Wells were caused to be dug by me every half krośa (or eight krośas);
- Resthouses (?) were constructed;
- Many watering stations were caused by me to be erected here and there for the benefit of beast and man.

(Guruge 1993 pp. 555 & 581)

Meritorious deeds to be performed, according to the Buddha's teachings, are (i) Charity or generous giving; (ii) Virtuous life; (iii) Development of the mind through meditation; (iv) Reverence to those worthy of reverence; (v) Service to the elderly, the needy, the sick and society at large; (vi) Transference of one's merits to others; (vii) Rejoicing in merits acquired by others; (viii) Expounding or teaching the Dhamma; (ix) Listening to the Dhamma; and (x) Straightening or rectifying one's views. There are four ways in which one treats one's fellow humans: (i) giving or generosity (*dāna*), (ii) kind and pleasant words (*piyavacana*), (iii) benevolent action (*atthacariyā*), and (iv) equality (*samānattatā*).

Merit-making as practiced by modern Buddhists gives an enormous fillip to the practice of the humanistic principles and values of Early Buddhism. Avoiding harm and injury to all sentient beings and working for their well-being comprise all forms of humane and social services. Feeding and clothing the poor and the orphaned, providing shelter to the homeless, educating the ignorant, caring for the sick and the destitute, providing communal amenities and the like are equivalent to religious obligations. "If one has nothing else to give others one could offer one's personal service," is an oft-quoted principle when people are organized to do community services. These are aptly called donations of effort or labor (*śramadāna*).

Thus is Grand Master Hsing Yun perfectly correct in asserting that Buddhism should not be equated with passivity or inactivity. The word for a Buddhist monastic, *Śramaṇa*, is derived from the root *śram* — to exert, to strive. The Buddha disapproved of people who ate immoderately, slept too long, were lazy and showed little energy (Dp. 7, 8). His ideal was the active and the diligent: The diligent will never die while those without diligence are already dead, he said in the Dhammapada (Dp. 21).

Self-liberation vs. Service to Others

"All compounded things are of the nature of decay. Accomplish your goal with diligence. Do not look back. Go forward" are the last words attributed to the Buddha (D. 16). This statement is taken in Southern Buddhism to emphasize the importance of self-liberation, meaning the attainment of enlightenment as a Buddha, a Paccekabuddha or a Śrāvaka. The life of a monastic who has renounced comforts and luxuries of household is held out as the ideal. Liberation is so urgent that the attainment of the status of an Arahant as a disciple is considered more than adequate. As Buddhism evolved, the monastic ideal was replaced in a popular tradition in India itself by the Bodhisattva ideal. A Bodhisattva is someone aspiring to become a Buddha.

One took the Bodhisattva vow to become a Buddha so that one not only liberated oneself but was also able to save others by leading them to liberation. As the attainment of Buddhahood was the highest achievement, the tradition which upheld this doctrine was known as the **Mahāyāna** — the Great Vehicle or Great Raft, as some modern scholars translate it. In a further development, the Bodhisattva vow further embodied the concept that a Bodhisattva deliberately delayed his self-liberation until he had seen to the salvation of every sentient being in the universe: In comparison, the ideal of enlightenment as a disciple attaining the status of an Arahant has been described in Mahāyāna texts with the disparaging term **Hīnayāna** — Lesser Vehicle or Smaller Raft.

Western scholars of the eighteenth and nineteenth centuries knew little of the intricacies of the Buddhist traditions and visualized them to have had as much a hostile and violent relationship as Roman Catholicism and Protestant Christianity. Accordingly, whatever differences found between the two main Buddhist traditions were exaggerated and explained in their own way. One such explanation is that Southern Buddhism upheld **Wisdom** whereas the Mahāyāna tradition ascribed primacy to **Compassion**. But, today, we know much more of the similarities and differences of the main traditions of Buddhism that we see no reason to posit such a black-and-white contrast. **Wisdom** and **Compassion** are not mutually exclusive Buddhist values. In actual Buddhist practice they are mutually reinforcing and intermingled.

I heard or read a long time ago a story whose source I have not been able to trace so far. It speaks of two monastics who had to reach a certain destination for a special purpose. As they proceeded on the route to this destination, they reached an extensive part of the road which was impassable on account of foul-smelling rubbish and human and animal waste. One monk set out to clean the road. He wanted the road to be cleared of obstacles so that other travelers would proceed on it. The other monk thought differently. He found some rags, bandaged his legs up to the knees, and waded through the stinking mess. Out on the other side, he removed his bandages, proceeded to his destination and fulfilled his purpose. After that, he returned to the fouled road and set about cleaning it. This story was supposed to compare and contrast the ideal of self-liberation of Early Buddhism and that of giving priority to the salvation of others. Which of the two monastics was wiser or more compassionate? Whose was the more reasonable course of action? Was the monastic who found a way to accomplish his own pre-determined purpose selfish and self-centered and hence to be criticized? Was the monastic who gave priority to serving the welfare of others to be praised? What if he served others and forfeited his own purpose? One may raise more questions. The debate would be interminable. In reality, both had service for others' well-being as an overall target and differed in only the priority each assigned.

In the light of this discussion, the Grand Master's comment on the importance of figuring out how to live as a human being in the human realm before proceeding on long retreats for self-liberation is apposite. He does not make the fulfillment of human obligations an alternative to self-liberation. He assigns importance to both but highlights how the fulfillment of human obligations is an essential pre-requisite for self-liberation. How very eloquently he reiterates his fundamental message!

- Remember, no one is going to achieve liberation from the cycle of birth and death if he has not figured out how to live as a human being in the human realm.
- All of us must live fully, virtuously and compassionately in this world before we can ever expect to transcend anything.
- If Buddhism is to develop as a viable religion in the world, it must adapt to conditions which are present in this world.
- Every choice made of the future of Buddhism should be founded on clear reasoning and good intentions.
- Humanistic Buddhism emphasizes our treatment of other people above everything else. No one can ever expect to come into full awareness of the Bodhi mind if they do not know how to treat other people with compassion, respect and unfailing kindness.

When viewed from such a perspective, Humanistic Buddhism is founded on both Wisdom and Compassion.

Precept and Example of *Śākyamuni* Buddha

Inspiration From the Historical Buddha

Grand Master Hsing Yun concludes his message to the First International Conference on Humanistic Buddha with a reference to the historical Buddha, the sage of the Śākyas:

> All Buddhists are living representatives of Śākyamuni Buddha, his teachings, and his compassion. Our basic faith comes from the Buddha himself. His teachings and his life are an example of truth, virtue, wisdom and perseverance. The Dharma is based on a reliance on our own innermost Buddha nature and the wisdom of our own inherent Bodhi mind. Through unity and compassion we will succeed in bringing Buddhism to all world's people.

All traditions of Buddhism speak of a multiplicity of Buddhas. A list of twenty-eight Buddhas beginning with Taṇhankara, Medhankara and Saraṇankara occurs in *Buddhavaṃsa* of the *Khuddakanikāya* and in a popular text in the *Paritta* or Book of Protection of Southern Buddhism. (Cf. *Aṭavisipirita*). A more widely circulated list is that of twenty-five, beginning with Dīpankara and including Gotama, the sage of the Śākyas.

In all Buddhist traditions, the first encounter of Śākyamuni Buddha with Dīpankara Buddha is the starting point of his quest for enlightenment. Śākyamuni in that life was an ascetic named Sumedha and had the opportunity to be enlightened as a disciple: that is, to be an Arahant under the guidance of Dīpankara Buddha. Instead he resolved to be a Buddha like Dīpankara and save humanity. All traditions agree that Śākyamuni Buddha's career as a Bodhisattva began with this resolution and Dīpankara Buddha's assurance of its accomplishment. *Prajñāpāramitā* has the Buddha to say,

> "So did I, when I met the Tathāgata Dīpankara in the bazaar of Dīpavatī, the royal city, possess the fullness of this perfection of wisdom, so that Dīpankara, the Tathāgata, predicted that one day I should be fully enlightened, and said to me: 'You, young Brahman, shall in a future period, after incalculable aeons, become a Tathāgata, Śākyamuni by name, — Endowed with knowledge and virtue, Well-Gone, a World-knower, Unsurpassed, Tamer of men to be tamed, Teacher of Gods and men, a Buddha, a Blessed Lord!'"

And again,

> "It was when I strewed the five lotus flowers over Dīpankara, the Tathāgata, and I acquired the patient acceptance of dharmas which fail to be produced, and then Dīpankara predicted my future enlightenment with the words: 'You, young man, will in a future period become a Tathāgata, Śākyamuni by name!'"

(Edward Conze [Tr.], 1973, pp. 102 & 220)

Even more graphically the Sinhala version stresses that the ascetic Sumedha abandoned the bliss of Nibbāṇa which was so near at hand (*atața pat nivan at hära*) and chose the long and arduous struggle for Buddhahood.

Postponing one's own liberation and striving to be a savior of humanity as a Bodhisattva for countless aeons of world cycles is what the majority of the Buddhists in the world uphold as the most significant example set to them by Śākyamuni Buddha. The intensity of self-effacing altruism and self-sacrifice, inherent in the postponement of one's liberation for the sake of others, has made the Bodhisattva ideal the more popular goal for this majority. They are stimulated by this episode to urge, "Let us do what the Buddha did rather than what he said." So do they choose the Bodhisattva vow:

> However numerous the beings are, I vow to save them.
> However inexhaustible the passions are, I vow to extinguish them.
> However immeasurable the doctrines are, I vow to master them.
> However incomparable the Buddha-truth is, I vow to attain it.
>
> (Guruge, 1999, p. 54)

The rich narrative literature of Buddhist traditions presents Śākyamuni Buddha's career as a Bodhisattva in hundreds of inspiring stories. The Jātaka literature as contained in the Pali commentary on *Jātaka* of the Pali Canon and *Jātakamālā*, the Sanskrit compila-tion of the Mahāyāna tradition, recounts many lives in which he practiced the ten or six perfections or Pāramitās. It is interesting to compare and contrast the two lists of Pāramitās:-

Northern Buddhism	Southern Buddhism
(i) ***Charity or Liberality***[17]	(i) ***Charity or Liberality***[17]
(ii) ***Virtue or Moral Precepts or Restraint***	(ii) ***Virtue or Moral Precepts or Restraint***
(iii) ***Forbearance, Patience or Tolerance***	(iii) Renunciation
(iv) ***Vigor, Effort or Energy***	(iv) ***Forbearance, Patience or Tolerance***

[17] Paramitas common to both traditions are in bold letters.

(v) Mental Concentration	(v) ***Vigor, Effort or Energy***
(vi) ***Wisdom***	(vi) ***Wisdom/Knowledge***
	(vii) Truthfulness
	(viii) Determination or Perseverance
	(ix) Loving Kindness
	(x) Equanimity

Five of the Pāramitās are common to both lists and it is possible that Wisdom or Knowledge of Southern Buddhism incorporates Mental Concentration. Northern Buddhism "sometimes adds four more Pāramitās: skilful means of teaching, power over obstacles, spiritual aspiration, and knowledge, these last four being, however, regarded as amplifications of *Prajñā*, wisdom" (Christmas Humphreys, 1976, p. 145-146).

Two later works in verse added to the Pali Canon concentrate on Śākyamuni's fulfillment of Pāramitās. *Buddhavaṃsa* provides brief biographical sketches of the Buddhas from Dīpankara to Śākyamuni. In it is described how the ten *Pāramitās* were practiced by Śākyamuni who, in the process, has met each of his twenty-four predecessors and had the assurance of his attaining Buddhahood. *Cariyāpiṭaka* deals with thirty-five existences of Śākyamuni as Bodhisattva in which he practiced seven *Pāramitās*. The missing three Pāramitās are Forbearance, Wisdom and Vigour (*Burma Piṭaka Association,* 1985 pp. 136-138).

All these not only depict the career of a Bodhisattva as one of utmost compassion but also highlight the highest esteem that is assigned to Buddhahood as the most desirable vehicle through which enlightenment, the end of suffering and the ultimate bliss of Nirvāṇa or Nibbāṇa, is to be achieved. It is not only in Northern Buddhism that Buddhahood is the ultimate goal but in Southern Buddhism, too, the basic wish of a devoted Buddhist is to become a Buddha. The most fervent way of expressing gratitude is to wish the doer of the good deed to be born as a Buddha (Guruge, 2000, p. 90).

The last life of Śākyamuni Buddha is as much a source of inspiration. All traditions accept and use in worship the ten or nine qualities of the Buddha as Worthy, Perfectly Enlightened, Endowed with knowledge and virtue, Well-gone, World-knower, Unsurpassed, Tamer of men to be tamed, Teacher of gods and men, Buddha, Blessed One.[18] His renunciation of royal luxury and power and adoption of a life of poverty — from regalia to rags — has touched the hearts of many generations of people even outside the Buddhist circles. His biography has been compiled and widely diffused in every tradition of Buddhism. The commentarial literature in Pali presents his life with few literary frills. Aśvaghoṣa wrote it in Sanskrit in the style of court poetry. Again in Sanskrit is *Lalitavistara* in which the supramundane elements overshadow the human. Chinese, Tibetans and Koreans have their own versions. In all these are highlighted the principal events and circumstances of his life:

- Royal ancestry
- Birth under a tree at Lumbini
- Prophesies on a career as a universal monarch or a religious leader
- A father's anxiety for a worthy successor
- A life of luxury, isolated from realities of existence
- The shocking discovery of sickness, old age and death
- The birth of a son
- The Great Departure
- Six years of study, penance and fasting
- The discovery of the Middle Path between the extremes of self-indulgence and self-mortification

---

[18] This is exactly the set of qualities as it occurs in many discourses of the Pali Canon as "*Iti pi so bhagavā araham sammāsambuddho vijjācaraṇasampanno sugato lokavidū anuttaro purisadammasārathī satthā devamanussānam buddho bhagavā ti.*" Cf. the identical text and order in the quote from *Prajñāpāramitā* with one omission. Missing from the list is *Arahaṃ* or Worthy. Could it be due to the Mahāyāna concept of Arahant as a lesser achievement? Mahādeva's questions already show that Arahant was considered less than perfect. Hence possibly the reluctance to recognize *Arahaṃ* as an epithet of the Buddha.

- The final struggle — a night of resolving conflicts, portrayed in literature and art as "the war against Māra"
- The attainment of Buddhahood and that, too, under a tree at Gaya
- The first sermon at Isipatana to five one-time colleagues in spiritual effort
- A mission of forty-five or forty-nine years:
  - preaching a doctrine of inner serenity and peace with equal enthusiasm to kings and princes, the rich and the poor, the scholar and the ignorant, the friendly and the hostile;
  - establishing the Sangha of bhikkhus and bhikkhuṇis as a self-renewing body of persons committed to discipline and service;
  - promoting an intellectual movement which gave humanity a stupendous treasure of prose and poetry covering ethics and philosophy, religious and social norms, exemplars for emulation and inspirational utterances to raise one's sagging spirit;
  - laying the foundation to a religious movement which influenced the diverse people of an entire continent for over twenty-five centuries;
  - handling hostilities, expressed verbally and in violent actions, with the calm conviction that loving-kindness and compassion would ultimately be victorious
- Death under the twin śāla trees at Kusinārā

The story is being retold in words and pictures, song and drama, in flimsy pamphlets and musty tomes, and in the language of the common people and the rhetorics and oratory of the learned. It has never ceased to capture the imagination of humanity.

For the first five hundred years, the deep veneration in which Śākyamuni Buddha was held by his disciples and followers would not allow him to be portrayed in sculpture or painting in the human form. Wherever a story needed his presence to be indicated, symbols alone were used: a bodhi-tree (*ficus religiosa*), a royal parasol, an empty seat, foot-prints, a wheel, or a column of fire. It was a foreign dynasty, the Kushans of Central Asian origin, that chose to represent Śākyamuni Buddha in human form. Starting with the gold coin of Kaniska I, where the standing figure of the Buddha is identified in Greek letters as BODDO, the image of the Buddha has had a remarkable history.

With no way to know what the Buddha looked like, each community has created its own Buddha image with its own criteria of physical beauty as well as intellectual and spiritual qualities. From Gandhara to Mathura, from Ajanta to Dunhuang and Loyang, from Sarnath to Sri Lanka, from Sokkuram to Kamakura, the image of the Buddha displays a wide diversity in artistic expression. Yet, in all locations, it continues to be a perfect symbol of the noblest qualities expressed in the teachings of Śākyamuni Buddha. It is not surprising at all that the Buddha holds the record for having the largest number of monuments and representations in art to commemorate his life and mission.

Śākyamuni Buddha continues to inspire people who come to know him. The impact he has in modern times may best be illustrated with my own personal experience in rediscovering my Buddhist heritage in adolescence.

Re-discovering My Buddhist Heritage (A Case Study)

Even before the teaching of religion in schools became universal, a child in a Sri Lankan home literally received his introduction to his spiritual heritage with the mother's milk. Thus, in a Buddhist home this induction took the form of visits to temples, veneration of and perhaps association with the Sangha, and participation in ceremonies and festivals. Progressively, the informal learning of Buddhist principles and values through popular narratives and poetry would be supplemented by formal study of the life of the Buddha, his main teachings and the history of Buddhism, usually in a Sunday school. Most children would pass through into adulthood with this initial grounding in Buddhism. As grown-ups they would give to charities, maintain institutions, support the Sangha and serve as the mainstay in the preservation of Buddhism as a living force in the country.

As opposed to the majority who had such a smooth transition, there were those whose adolescence exposed them to new and, in many ways, disturbing influences. Either they went to schools where a different spiritual background was provided or their intellectual curiosity led them to insights and experiences which stimulated skepticism. In either case, the new knowledge which one gained at this stage in science and philosophy, history and economics — specially of the western world — infused a sense of intellectual independence, bordering on superiority. To question one's own heritage or even to treat it somewhat nonchalantly or disparagingly would, unconsciously, become a fashion. The reinforcement of such attitudes came from one's peer-group which invariably applauded the more eloquent of the rebels. One fancied oneself to be a rationalist and decried belief and faith. Only **reason** mattered, one would argue.

I recall my own adolescence in the 1940s, when, under the influence of the then most popular Thinker's Library and the Left Book Club, the national cultural heritage was continually being reappraised. What was thus re-evaluated included the entire gamut of values and practices, religious and aesthetic as well as social and political. Every question which appeared to cause embarrassment to elders gave a particular sense of satisfaction. **Revolt** had its own pleasures, mainly intellectual.

In my case, the requisite jolt came from a Buddhist monk of Dutch origin, who explained how he came to embrace Buddhism. He had been impressed with assessments which some European scholars had made of Buddhism. He quoted three of the favorite authors of the time — H.G. Wells, Bertrand Russell and Carl Gustav Jung — men whose credentials as "rationalists" or "modern thinkers" were highly regarded by us.

To Wells was ascribed the statement that "*Buddhism has done more for the advance of world civilization and true culture than any other influences in the chronicles of mankind.*"

Russell had been more specific. He had said, "*Buddhism is a combination of both speculative and scientific philosophy. It advocates the scientific method and pursued that to a finality that may be called rationalistic. In it are to be found answers to such questions of interest as 'What are mind and matter? Is the Universe moving towards a goal? What is man's position? Is there living that is noble?' It takes up where science cannot lead because of the limitations of the latter's instruments. Its conquests are those of the mind.*"

Unequivocal in his appreciation of Buddhism was Jung, one-time colleague and later adversary of Sigmund Freud. Jung asserted, "*As a student of comparative religion, I believe that Buddhism is the most perfect one the world has ever seen. The philosophy of the Buddha, the theory of evolution and the Law of Karma were far superior to any other creed.*"

I was impressed too — specially impressed and even proud of this great religion. It has been so highly rated by men whose intellectual achievements my generation almost worshipped. More also, it had come to me as my birthright, my natural heritage. I could not help but admit that I was born lucky to inherit such a valued treasure.

A search for further confirmation resulted in the discovery of other equally encouraging assertions. Max Muller, an eminent scholar of Eastern cultures, whom the Western world hailed as the father of Indological Studies, called the Buddha's moral code "*the most perfect the world has ever seen.*" Viggo Fausboll, the Danish scholar who was among the earliest to translate a Buddhist text for a western audience — namely, **Dhammapada** into Latin in 1855 — expressed his accord with the statement on the Buddha: "*The more I know him, the more I love him.*"

The Marquis of Zetland, a Viceroy of India, in a learned article on India's democratic traditions, said, "*It is indeed to the Buddhist books that we have to turn for an account of the manner in which the affairs of these early examples of representative self-governing institutions were conducted. And it may come as a surprise to many to learn that in the assemblies of Buddhists in India two thousand years and more ago were to be found the rudiments of our own parliamentary practice of the present day.*"

Similarly inspiring was an assessment by T. W. Rhys Davids, the pioneering Pali and Buddhist scholar to whom the West owes its in-depth knowledge of Buddhist literature and philosophy. He wrote: "*There is no record, known to me in the whole of the long history of Buddhism through the many centuries where its followers have been for such lengthened periods supreme, of any persecution of any other* ***faith***."

Other heroes of our adolescent days proved to be equally enthusiastic admirers of the Buddha and his teachings. Among them was the youthful Indian leader, Jawaharlal Nehru — biologist by training and rationalist by attitude in the vanguard in the struggle for independence. Not only did he take with him to jail a picture of the Samādhi statue of Anuradhapura but also wrote of it in his autobiography: "*I kept it on my little table in my cell. It became a precious companion for me, and the strong, calm features of the Buddha's statue soothed and gave me strength and helped me to overcome many a period of depression.*"

He was in a way confirming what the philosopher P. D. Ouspensky had already observed: "*I began to feel the strange effect which the Buddha's face produced on me. All the gloom that rose from the depth of my soul seemed to clear up. It was as if the Buddha's face communicated its calm to me. Everything that up to now had troubled me and appeared so serious and important, now became small, insignificant and unworthy of notice, that I only wondered how it could ever have affected me. And I felt that no matter how agitated, troubled, irritated and torn with contradictory thoughts and feelings a man might be when he came here, he would go away calm, quiet, enlightened, understanding.*"

This exceedingly favorable impression of the Buddha and Buddhism was further enhanced by a group of European and American writers who saw in Buddhism a spiritual ally to scientific development. Prominent among them, the German scholar, Paul Dalkhe wrote so very convincingly on Buddhism in relation to modern science. He said, "*Buddhism, alone, among all world reli-*

gions, stands in not ***a priori*** *contradiction to scientific thought*" and "*It is true there breathes about this system something of the coldness of mathematics; on the other hand, there lives in it that purest and sublimest beauty, that taintless beauty, which belongs only to mathematics.*"

It was one thing to be pleased with what others had said so very admiringly of one's cultural and spiritual heritage; but a quite different thing to be convinced that all the praise was rightly deserved. It became intellectually an exciting experience to inquire how Buddhism earned all this praise from so varied types of personalities. The inquiry has lasted all my life. I have devoted most of my leisure over five decades to pursuing studies on various aspects of the religion and the culture which the teachings of the Buddha inspired.

The more knowledge I gained, the greater grew my admiration of not only this magnificent heritage to which I have become an heir, but also my ancestors who in diverse ways sought to preserve it for us. It has been a remarkable **rediscovery** of my own heritage — something that I nearly lost in the ebullience of adolescent revolt. But the fact that it has been a rediscovery achieved through the dint of study and inquiry, thought and meditation makes it much more valuable and meaningful than if it was a tacit conformity with traditional belief and ritual. Mine is thus a heritage which I have truly made mine.

Ever since, I have this message of hope and admiration to place before doubting and inquiring adolescents:

> May your search be as fruitful, inspiring and rewarding as mine has been! True to the Buddha's own confidence in the efficacy of his Path, Buddhism stands up to any stringent investigation. No wonder that the most remarkable epithet given to his teachings was '**Ehipassika**' — come and see for yourselves. The best reward for a comprehensive study of Buddhism — the religion and its culture — comes from the realization that it brings one face to face with some of the noblest creations of human-

> kind in ethics and philosophy, art and architecture, logic and poetry.
>
> (Guruge, 1993-1, pp. 208-211)

So have we to agree wholeheartedly with Grand Master Hsing Yun's appraisal that Buddhists are — and, if not, should equip themselves to be — living representatives of Śākyamuni Buddha. In spite of his modest declaration that he was only the discoverer of a lost city and an old path leading to it (*Saṃyutta-nikāya* XII, 65 — *Nagarasutta*), the historical Buddha is the founder of Buddhism. Without him this rich and varied religious system would not have come into existence. His fundamental teachings are universally recognized as indispensable to every tradition, school or sect. They are the most sought after by the scholar and the devotee to understand the unity in diversity of Buddhism.

Essential Doctrines: Unity in Diversity

Ever since Śākyamuni Buddha came to the attention of the modern Western scholars nearly two hundred years ago, they have assiduously searched for the kernel of common Buddhist beliefs and principles in different traditions.

In 1891, the American Theosophist, Colonel Henry Steel Olcott, identified a fourteen-item "common platform upon which all Buddhists can agree." Item (V) of the document reads:

> "Sākya Muni taught that ignorance produces desire, unsatisfied desire is the cause of rebirth, and rebirth the cause of sorrow. To get rid of sorrow, therefore, it is necessary to escape rebirth; to escape rebirth, it is necessary to extinguish desire; and to extinguish desire, it is necessary to destroy ignorance."

Another attempt in the same direction was made by Christmas Humphreys in 1945. Called "Twelve Principles of Buddhism," his analysis aims at reconciling the views of different schools. As regards the basic teaching, he laid stress on the following:

> "Life being one, the interests of the part should be those of the whole. In his ignorance man thinks

he can successfully strive for his own interests, and this wrongly directed energy to selfishness produces suffering. He learns from his suffering to reduce and finally eliminate its cause. The Buddha taught four Noble Truths: (a) the omnipresence of suffering; (b) its cause, wrongly directed desire; (c) its cure, the removal of the causes; and (d) the Noble Eightfold Path of self-development which leads to the end of suffering.

The Eightfold Path consists in Right (or Perfect) Views or preliminary understanding, Right Aims or Motives, Right Speech, Right Acts, Right Livelihood, Right Efforts, Right Concentration or mind-development, and, finally, Right *Samadhi*[20], leading to full Enlightenment. As Buddhism is a way of living, not merely a theory of life, the treading of this Path is essential to self-deliverance. 'Cease to do evil, learn to do good, cleanse your own heart; this is the teaching of the Buddhas.' The Buddha was the All-Compassionate as well as the All-Enlightened One."

(Both documents are reproduced in full in Guruge, 1999, pp. 79-83)

The most recent and consequently the most comprehensive is the 1997 declaration of the American Buddhist Congress and Southern California Sangha Council of USA under the leadership of Venerable Dr. Havanpola Ratanasara, entitled "Ten-point Convention on Buddhism Across Cultures."[21] It runs as follow:

---

[20] *Sammāsati* is now translated by most scholars as Right Mindfulness and *Sammasamādhi* as Right Concentration. Some tend to translate *Sammāsati* as Right Mind, which is inadequate because the significance of *sati* or *smṛti* as emphasized in *Satipaṭṭhāna Sutta* or *Saddharmasmṛtyupasthāna Sūtra* is lost in the process. The other elements of the Noble Eightfold Path are also translated differently by scholars. But the need for fixed terminology has yet to be recognized.

[21] The drafting committee comprised Havanpola Ratanasara, Ananda W.P. Guruge, Karuna Dharma, Henry Shin and Jack Bath.

1. We recognize Śākyamuni Gautama Buddha as the historical source for the transmission of Buddha Dharma of our time and venerate him for his compassionate service to humanity.
2. We recognize the multiplicity of the Buddhas of the past, the present and the future, as well as Pacceka (pratyeka) Buddhas, Arahants and Bodhisattvas.
3. We take refuge in the Triple Gem consisting of the Buddha, the Dharma, and the Sangha.
4. We aspire to the fruits of enlightenment and liberation from *dukkha* (suffering) for others and ourselves in a spirit of compassion to all beings.
5. We hold, as central to the spirit and goals of Buddhism:
   a. The Four Noble Truths: Suffering (*dukkha*), cause of suffering (*samudaya*), cessation of Suffering (*nirodha*) and the Path to the cessation of suffering (*dukkhanirodhagāmiṇīpaṭipadā*);
   b. The three signata: impermenence (*anicca* or *anitya*); suffering or unsatisfactoriness (*dukkha* or *duḥkha*); and non-self or insubstantiality (*anatta* or *anātman*);
   c. The Noble Eightfold Path (*Ariya Aṭṭhangika Magga*) consisting of Right Thought, Right Motive, Right Speech, Right Action, Right Livelihood, Right Effort, Right Mindfulness and Right Concentration;
   d. Twelve Links of Dependent Origination (*Paticcasamuppada* or *pratītyasamutpāda*);
   e. The three stages of Buddhist development: ethical conduct (*sīla*), one-pointed mental concentration (*samādhi*), and wisdom (*paññā* or *prajñā*); and
   f. The four sublime or immeasurable states: loving-kindness (*metta* or *maitri*), compassion

(*karuṇā*), sympathetic joy (*muditā*) and equanimity (*upekkhā* or *upekṣā*);

6. We accept our moral responsibility for the results of what we think, say or do, and subscribe to the principles of *karma* and its outcome (*vipāka*).
7. We share a commitment to make every effort to conform to the ethical ideals of Buddhism of avoiding all unwholesome action, doing wholesome actions and keeping the mind pure by:
    a. Abstaining from killing, stealing, sexual misconduct, lying, harsh speech, idle talk, slander, stupefying intoxicants, covetousness, anger and malice, and deluded thoughts;
    b. Practicing caring with loving-kindness, generosity, contentment, truthfulness, kind speech, meaningful talk, harmonious speech, temperance, and generous, compassionate and clear thoughts;
    c. Eradicating the root causes of unskillful action: greed (*lobha*), hatred (*dosa* or *dveṣa*), and delusion (*moha*).
8. We recognize the potentiality of every being to attain enlightenment from the cycle of birth and death (*saṃsāra*) in *Nibbāṇa* (*Nirvāṇa*) and we accept the validity and effectiveness of different paths leading to final emancipation.
9. We realize that the conventional expressions of truth and reality are manifold; and, in the light of Śākyamuni Buddha's own guidelines for an open-minded and tolerant quest for the Ultimate Truth, recognize the importance of deferring to inter-traditional differences and practices of the Buddha Dharma.
10. We uphold our commitment to tolerance, compassion and mutual understanding within and among our diverse traditions, as well as between us

and the religious and secular communities outside our traditions and, in order to foster a collective effort towards global, harmonious spiritual development, undertake

a. To study and appreciate one another's teachings, religious and social practices and cultural heritage;
b. To avoid imposing our beliefs through coercion, manipulation or force, and
c. To utilize every opportunity for dialogue and cooperation.

It is such a comprehensive approach to the doctrinal unity of all traditions of Buddhism that Grand Master Hsing Yun advocates as the foundation of Humanistic Buddhism. Hence does he stress that "our basic faith comes from the Buddha himself" and that "his teachings and his life are an example of truth, virtue, wisdom and perseverance." How apt is the Grand Master's vision: "Through unity and compassion we will succeed in bringing Buddhism to all world's people."

Humanistic Buddhism in a Changing World

A Buddhist Systems Approach

In this chapter we direct our attention to Grand Master Hsing Yun's vision of the world today. In the same message we have so far analyzed, he says,

> The world is changing quickly. To grasp these changes and use them for our good, we must fully comprehend the inter-workings of societies, science, economics, governments and the environment. If Buddhism is to develop as a viable religion in the world, it must adapt itself to the conditions which are present in this world. Every choice we make of the future of Buddhism should be founded on clear reasoning and good intentions. The path of the Arhant has its Four Directions and Four Fruits, while the Bodhisattva Way of Mahayana is divided into fifty-two detailed stages. These details and divisions show the importance that Buddhism places on clarity of vision and good planning.

Śākyamuni Buddha's success when he was alive and the ever-expanding success of Buddhism ever since is heavily dependent on the systems approach which he adopted. **Systems approach** is a modern, technical term applied in management and operations research. It is based on the view that every system — from the universe to the smallest human activity — consists of interdependent and interacting sub-systems or components. No activity, however minute, can be planned, organized, directed or controlled until and unless (i) the relationships among the components are understood, and (ii) the effect which changes in one component have on each of the others is carefully evaluated.

The Grand Master advocates such a systems approach and identifies the following as the important components of the modern world: societies (under which are subsumed such elements of society as social organization and conditions, family values, gender issues, and culture), economics, governments, the environment and science. From his vantage position as the head of a world-wide congregation supported by a most impressive religious and educational infrastructure, he is conscious of the fundamental importance of adaptation to prevailing conditions and of making choices in the process. He also knows from experience that compliance to conditions is no virtue. In the same message he says,

> "Buddhists were too often content to 'follow conditions' and not create them themselves. Without a vision of our future, Buddhism will continue to languish in its cocoon, and by doing that, fundamentally contradict some of its most basic principles."

If the Grand Master suggests that one swims against the current, he also adds the caveat that reaching the further shore must be the uncompromising objective.

The Buddha's Views on Societies, Government, Economics and Environment

<u>*Equality of Human Beings*</u>

Śākyamuni Buddha had something to say on every aspect of human life. He reacted to social inequalities of his day and preached that moral conduct alone and not birth or wealth would make one human being "more equal than" another. He confronted prominent Brahmans and convinced them of the futility of their claims of superiority. As we have already seen, the Buddha was not merely a man of words. He was a man of action. The Sangha is founded on the ideals of social, economic and inter-personal equality that he sought for the whole world. The untouchable scavenger and the despised prostitute had a place in it. The humble barber was accorded precedence over his one-time royal masters. Arrogance and vanity had to give way to serenity and compassion.

The underlying doctrine of the equality of all human beings is sorely needed today to counteract prevailing social evils of intolerance, bigotry, exploitation and ever-worsening conditions of the poor, the disadvantaged and the under-privileged. The problems which are grappled with are more complex. So, as the Grand Master envisages in his concept of Humanistic Buddhism, the teachings of the Buddha have to be reinterpreted to apply to our times.

For example, the Buddha analyzed the causes of anarchy and violence in *Kūṭadantasutta* (D. 5) and identified poverty as the foremost underlying cause. Therefore he argued against law-enforcement and punishment as effective solutions:

> "Perchance his majesty might think, 'I will soon put a stop to these scoundrels' game by degradation and punishment, and fines and imprisonment and execution.' But the criminal actions of bandits who pillage villages and towns and make roads unsafe cannot be satisfactorily put a stop to. The criminals left unpunished would still go on harassing the realm. Now there is one method to adopt to put a thorough end to this disorder: to those who keep cattle and cultivate farms, let the king give fodder and seed-corn. To those who trade, let the king give capital. To those in government service, let the king give wages and food. Then these people, following each one's own business, will no longer harass the realm. The king's revenue will go up and the realm will be quiet and at peace. The

populace, pleased with one another and happy, dancing their children in their arms, will dwell with open doors." (D. 5)

Government subsidies to the private sector and adequate salaries to service personnel so as to ensure an economically viable society are the proffered answers to the problem of economic instability and resulting violence. These are valid measures even today, as crime has its origin in poverty and ignorance.

Similarly, issues pertaining to gender conflict find in Buddhism a basis on which re-thinking to suit modern times could be embarked on. The Buddha's advice on the equality of women has a perennial validity; he told the king Pasenadi of Kosala:

"A woman child, O lord of men, may prove
Even a better offspring than a male.
For she may grow up wise and virtuous,
Her husband's mother reverencing, true wife.
The boy she may bear may do great deeds,
And rule great realms, yea, such a son
Of noble wife becomes his country's guide."

(*Samyuttanikāya*. III, 2, 6)

In his list of seven factors which contributed to the security and development of a nation, the fourth was that women and girls should be assured protection from harassment. (D. 16).

After repeated refusal by the Buddha to ordain his step-mother, Ānanda asked the compelling question, "Are the women folk capable of going forth from home to homelessness in the Dhamma as preached by the Buddha and attaining the status of a Stream-Enterer, Once-Returner, Non-Returner or Arahant?" The answer of the Buddha was a categorical "Yes." Not only did he say so, but created the Order of Nuns to accommodate women, even though he set additional rules for them (*Cullavagga*. X,1). Of course, the first of the eight rules which makes the most senior nun junior to the just ordained monk has not been convincingly explained. Yet the step-mother as a nun was declared the chief of those with the longest experience (*Anguttaranikāya*. I, 25). In a non-Canonical work, *Manorathapūraṇī*, the spirit of the Buddhist attitude occurs as "Not on all occasions are men wise. Women, too, are wise and intelligent on various occasions." (*Itthī'pi paṇḍitā honti tattha tattha vicakkhaṇā*) (Vol. I, p.205).

How the Grand Master concurs with the foregoing appraisal of women by the Buddha is demonstrated by the role which nuns play in the hierarchy of the Fo Guang Shan Buddhists Order. There is no activity in which their superior talents are not amply utilized in serving the welfare of people.

The position of woman as **wife and mother** finds special mention in the Pali Canon. In several texts the mother is called the *pubbācariyā* or first teacher. Tending father and mother as well as wife and children are viewed as a blessing in the *Mahāmangala-sutta* (*Suttanipāta*, II, 16). A monk is not only permitted to share the food obtained by begging with one's parents but doing so is commended as an act praised by the wise (*paṇḍitā idh'eva naṃ pasaṃsanti*). (*Mātuposakasutta*, *Samyuttanikāya*, VII, 2, 9)

"The wife is one's best friend" (*bhariyā ca paramā sakhā*) is a dictum of the Buddha (Ibid. 6, 4). In an insightful analysis of the role and behavior of a wife in a marriage, he identifies as many as seven different kinds of wives. Three kinds he condemns as harsh and devoid of virtue and love: namely,

> torturing wife (*vadhakabhariyā*),
> stealing wife (*coribhariyā*) and
> domineering wife (*ayyabhariyā*).

Four others whom he praises are

> mother-wife (*mātubhariyā*), who is protective and tends a husband as a mother does a son,
> sister-wife (*bhaginibhariyā*) who is modest and respectful to the husband,
> friend-wife (*sakhībhariyā*), who is noble and chaste, and rejoices at the sight of the husband, and
> slave-wife (*dāsībhariyā*), who is free from anger and with a pure heart waits on the husband.

(*Anguttaranikāya*, VII, 59)

With such a knowledge and understanding of the relationship between husband and wife, the Buddha spelled out their mutual duties and obligations:

> "The **husband** fulfilled his duties toward the wife by respecting her, by not humiliating her, by being faithful, by handing over authority, and by presenting jewelry."

The last of the duties coincides with an analysis elsewhere in the Buddhist literature of "the insatiable desires of a woman" as sexual satisfaction, birth of children, and ornaments and jewelry.

> "The **wife** in turn performs her duties well, extends hospitality to relatives all around (i. e. to hers as well as her husband's), is faithful to her husband, protects what is earned and acquired, and is proficient and industrious in all duties."

(*Sigalovādasutta* D. 31)

Similarly duties and obligations of parents and children were analyzed as follow:

> "The **parents** are required to prevent the child from evil, inculcate good qualities, have the child taught an art (i.e. given an education leading to a livelihood), contract a marriage with a suitable partner, and hand over the inheritance in time. The **child** in return has to nourish them in their old age, perform his or her duties toward them, preserve the family and clan (that is, by procreation), protect the heritage, and make offerings when they are dead and gone." (Ibid)

Taking together the duties between parents and children and between husband and wife, the picture that emerges as the Buddha's ideal of family values and relations confirms deep concern in the stability of the home as the primary unit of society.

Government

The Buddha had views on government, too. He was equally close to practically all the kings who ruled various kingdoms in the region in which he was active. Though there is no evidence of his having played any direct role in statecraft, he was conscious of separating matters of state from those of religion. For example, no one was permitted to become a monk if he was under obligation to perform any royal duties (*Mahāvagga*, I, 4, 40). When the rising power of Magadha threatened the independence of the tiny Republic of the Vajjis, the Buddha assured them that no harm would come to them as long as they adhered to seven principles. With interpretations within parenthesis relevant to modern times, these principles demonstrate another instance of the Buddha's concern with human welfare:

1. Meet frequently in harmony, discuss in harmony and disperse in harmony. (That is, *participate fully in public life and affairs, observe the democratic principles of consultation, and preserve harmony in spite of differences*).
2. Introduce no revolutionary laws, do not break the established law, and abide by the old-time norm (That is, *to make a balance between the tradition and the modern, and make changes slowly and cautiously and not drastically.*)
3. Honor, reverence, esteem and worship the elders and deem them worthy of listening to. (That is, *recognize the value and relevance of trans-generational wisdom.*)
4. Safeguard the women-folk from force, abduction and harassment. (That is, *recognize the importance of women and their need for protection.*)
5. Honor, revere, esteem and worship both inner and outer shrines. (That is, *protect the cultural and spiritual heritage.*)
6. Perform without neglecting the customary offerings, (That is, *safeguard the practice of religion.*) and
7. So assure that saints have access to one's territory and having entered dwell there pleasantly. (That is,

be open to all religions and spiritual influences in a spirit of tolerance).

In later Buddhist literature in Pali occurs frequently a list of ten traditional duties of a ruler (*Dasa-rāja-dhamma*). They are i. Giving alms, ii. Virtuous life or morality, iii. Liberality, iv. Straightness or honesty, v. Gentleness, vi. Self-control (lit. asceticism), vii. Non-anger or pleasant temperament, viii. Nonviolence, ix. Forbearance, x. Non-opposition (*Jātaka*, I, 260, 399; II, 400). A list of three things to be avoided by a ruler consists of falsehood, anger and derisive laughter (Ibid. V, 120). The democratic norms which the Buddha adopted for decision-making and conflict-resolution within the Sangha, as discussed earlier, highlight his faith in government by compromise and consensus.

Economics

The Buddha was mindful of the place of economics in lay life. His advice to Sigāla as regards the handling of **money** is worthy of attention. Not only is he counseled to accumulate wealth for the benefit of the family as a bee collects pollen (i. e. without oppression to the producer of such wealth) but also to see wisely that the wealth grows high like an anthill. Such wealth has to be utilized as follows:

Divide the income into four,
Binding one's self to friends,
With one part may you enjoy (**consume**):
Invest two parts in your business.
Save the fourth, so that
It is there in times of distress. (D. 31)

Having money and being wealthy are not decried in the teachings of the Buddha, even though "wanting the least" (*appicchatā*) is highly recommended and contentment is commended as the highest wealth: *Santuṭṭhī paramaṃ dhanaṃ* (Dp. 204). Of course, there are the accounts of Sudinna and Raṭṭhapāla whose parents tried to tempt them with wealth to abandon monkhood. Their reply was that the parents should put all their wealth into bags, transport them in carts, and drop them into river Gangā where it was the deepest

(*Suttavibhanga*. I, 5 and M. 82). Poverty, thus, is appreciated when chosen by monastics. **Acquiring wealth** in the youth, nevertheless, is declared in the Dhammapada as an alternative to life as a monastic:

> "Those, who have not led the holy life [or] not acquired wealth in youth, pine away like old herons at a dry pond without fish or lie like worn-out bows, sighing after the past."
>
> (Dp. 155-156)

Prosperity in this life is regarded as a reward for good *Kamma* (Sanskrit *Karma*) in previous lives as well as the present. In one listing, **the possession of wealth** is said to generate four kinds of happiness for the laity; namely,

- happiness of having (*atthisukha*),
- happiness of consuming (*bhogasukha*),
- happiness of being free from debt (*ananasukha*), and
- happiness of blameless conduct (*anavajjasukha*).

(*Anguttaranikāya*. II, 62)

In *Vyagghapajjasutta*, Dighajānu asks the Buddha for advice for people like him who were encumbered with wives and children, used to luxuries like imported perfume, handled silver and gold and decked themselves with garlands, perfumes and unguents. The Buddha's response was to list four achievements each to ensure happiness in this life and hereafter. As regards this life, he enumerated the following:

1. persistent effort (*uṭṭhānasampadā*)
2. security and wariness (*ārakkhasampadā*)
3. good friendship (*kalyāṇamittatā*) and
4. balanced livelihood (*samajivikatā*)

The explanation of items 1, 2, and 4 elaborates the Buddha's views on wealth:

> Persistent effort: "By whatever activity a person earns his livelihood, whether by cultivation, animal husbandry, archery (=military service), ministering to kings or any other craft, one is skillful and not lazy,

reasons out to ways and means of accomplishing the tasks and is efficient and capable."

Security and wariness: "Whatever wealth a person has justly acquired by dint of effort, strength of arms, the sweat of the brow, or any other right means, one protects it by guarding and watching that kings would not seize it, thieves would not steal it, fire would not burn it, water would not carry it off or ill-disposed heirs would not take it away."

Balanced livelihood: "Knowing his income and expenditure, one leads a balanced life without being either too extravagant or too niggardly, thinking, 'My income can be in excess of my expenditure but not my expenditure in excess of income.' Just as a goldsmith or his apprentice knows by holding up a balance that by so much it has dipped down and by so much it has tilted up, one knows his income and expenditure and leads a balanced livelihood."

These principles tally with the definition of Right Livelihood (*sammā ājīva*) as one of the elements of the Noble Eightfold Path. The kinds of livelihood which are declared wrong as they bring harm to others include trading in arms, living beings, intoxicants and poison; slaughtering animals and fishing; soldiering, deceit, treachery, soothsaying, trickery, and usury. (Nyanatiloka: Buddhist Dictionary s.v. *Magga*)

As important as these statements in the Pali Canon on the Buddha's position regarding money and wealth are the accounts of very close friendships that he maintained with rich and generous donors like Anīthapiṇḍika and Visākhā. No further proof is needed to dispel the notion that either the Buddha or Buddhism scorned wealth or the wealthy.

The Buddha did, of course, advocate simplicity of life. While disapproving stinginess and miserliness, he praised generosity and thriftiness with equal emphasis. The story of the Buddha's personal physician, Jīvaka, includes an episode where a wealthy client orders her servant to save from the floor a drop of oil. She explains that it could be put to some useful purpose and, therefore should not be wasted. With equal emphasis on the importance of not wasting resources, another Buddhist story explains how a robe donated to the Buddha or the Sangha was diligently recycled until the shredded rag was mixed with mortar to repair a wall of a monastic building.

The Buddhist point of view about wealth and consumption is best summarized by Emperor Asoka. In Rock Edict III, he says,

> Commendable is to spend little (*apavyayatā)* and possess few things (*apabhaḍatā*).
>
> (Guruge, 1993, p. 556)

Related to economics is the treatment meted out to employees. Again in the *Sigālovādasutta* (D. 31) is the set of duties and obligations of employers and servants. Though restricted to household servants at the time of the Buddha, the obligations of each party are valid for employer-employee relations in general as will be shown by comments in parenthesis. The **employer** has to

- assign work according to strength or capacity (no king-size jobs for man-size employees, as the popular saying goes)
- provide food and salary (no enforced or unpaid labor)
- ensure health care (a specific obligation of the employer)
- share special delicacies (both as a demonstration of human concern and as recognition of good work: e. g. bonuses, perquisites and rewards), and
- grant leave at times (i. e. periods of rest as earned leave).

The **employee** in return wakes up earlier and sleeps later than the employer, is content with the wages and rewards given, does his or her work well and diligently, praises the employer and spreads his or her fame (i. e. subscribes to good public relations). How the Buddha's view persisted and had an impact nearly three centuries later is once again revealed by Emperor Asoka's edicts:

- "Good behavior towards slaves and servants" as a rite of Dharma (Rock Edict IX)
- "Proper treatment of slaves and servants" as the first of four items in his code of ethics (Rock Edict XI)
- "Good conduct and firm devotion to... slaves and servants" as a quality which the Emperor appreciated in virtuous people (Rock Edict XIII)

(Guruge, 1993, pp. 565, 566, 568)

Ecology and Environment

Ecology and environment is another concern deeply engrained in Grand Master Hsing Yun's concept of Humanistic Buddhism. His year-long campaign in 1998 to raise the awareness of Buddhists of nature and life began with the keynote address to the BLIA 7th General Conference in Canada. In it he said, "The natural world is our great body. We are it and it is us... the nature is truth, nature is the Buddhadharma, nature is the inherent goodness that lies within all of us, nature is the fullness and the culmination of the being of all things... We have based ourselves on the laws of nature as they were explained by Śākyamuni Buddha." (Nature and Life, BLIA, LA Chapter, Hacienda Heights, CA, 1998, pp. 23-24)

The Buddha was a lover of nature. He spent long periods in forests, in caves and under trees and encouraged his monastics to do so. The rules of discipline for monastics deal with measures for the conservation of nature. Strict prohibitions exist as regards polluting water resources with human waste; cutting down trees and branches thereof; and wandering around in seasons when wild life is likely to be trampled. Monastics are forbidden to use objects like needle-boxes made of bone, ivory or horn. The admonitions on killing are specific:

All beings fear violence (*daṇḍā*)
For life is precious to all
Comparing your own self
Do not kill; do not get others to kill

(Dp. 129 & 130, See also *Saṃyuttanikāya* XIX, 1459)

Monastics are warned to be careful even when drinking water which may have insects and tiny creatures. Forest dwelling monks who were harmed by wildlife or lived in fear of them were taught a special meditation to wish them well:

> Creatures without feet have my love,
> And likewise those that have two feet,
> And those that have four feet I love,
> And those, too, that have many feet.
> May those without feet harm me not,
> And those with two feet cause no hurt;
> May those with four feet harm me not,
> Nor those who many feet possess.
> Let creatures all, all things that live,
> All beings of whatever kind,
> See nothing that will bode them ill!
> May naught of evil come to them!
>
> (*Cullavagga*, V. 6)

On the positive side, the Buddha encouraged people to plant trees, protect forests and provide an environment beneficial to humans and beasts:

> Those who grow trees in forests and gardens which yield flowers and fruits, and bushes, build bridges, water houses, wells, and shelters as public services, they are worth earning merits, prosper at all times, are perfected with morality and righteousness and will finally go to heaven.
>
> (*Samyuttanikāya*, XV, 146)

Mention was already made of what Emperor Asoka had recorded as his public services in Rock Edict II and Pillar Edict VII. That they are in pursuit of the Buddha's own instructions is quite clear.

More in line of protecting the environment is Asoka's most impressive decree granting sanctuary to endangered species and setting guidelines on related subjects. His Pillar Edict V prohibits killing 21 named species as well as "bulls set at liberty, household pets and all quadrupeds who are neither utilized nor eaten." It also contains such provisions as the following:

1. She-goats, ewes and sows that are either pregnant or suckling the young are not to be killed; nor should their offspring up to six months.
2. Cocks are not to be caponized.
3. Husks with living creatures should not be burnt.
4. Forests should not be burnt without a purpose or to harm.
5. The living should not be nourished with the living.

Besides, the killing of all living creatures, including fish, is forbidden on prescribed holy days. So are castrating of bulls, goats or rams and branding horses and bulls (Guruge, 1993, p. 578). Repeated in every major Rock Edict is the injunction or information:

- One should take pity on living creatures (Minor Rock Edict II — both versions)
- The king abstains from killing animals and all men including the king's huntsmen and fishermen have stopped hunting and fishing (Minor Rock Edict IV in Greek and Aramaic)
- Commendable is abstention from killing living beings (Rock Edict III, See also RE IX, XI)
- Due to the king's admonitions have increased the abstention from slaughter of living creatures, and non-violence to beings (Rock Edict III)
- Various favors up to the granting of life have been done by me for quadrupeds, birds and aquatic animals. (Pillar Edict II)

(Guruge 1993, pp. 549, 550, 552, 556, 557, 565, 566, 574)

Indicative of a continuing commitment to biodiversity on the part of Buddhists is the decree of Āmaṇḍagāmiṇi (19-29 CE) who declared the whole island of Sri Lanka a non-killing zone (*Māghāta*).

Emphasized in some of the discourses of Early Buddhism is the concept that the environment became unfavorable and unsatisfactory as a result of the moral deterioration of the human being. (Cf. *Aggaññasutta* of *Dīghanikāya* D. 127 and *Brāhmaṇadhammikasutta* of *Khuddakanikāya*: *Suttanipāta* II, 19). Similarly was developed the concept that a righteous or unrighteous ruler could have a good or bad impact on environment. Quoted by Donald K. Swearer is a passage from the thirteenth century Thai classic, *Traibhūmikathā* by King Lithai of Sukhodaya, to illustrate how a ruling monarch subscribed to the tradition:

> "The grain, the water, fish and food, gems and precious ornaments, the seven gems and nine gems, silver and gold as well as silk and satin will be plentiful. The devatā will make the rain fall in the right season and the right amount, not too much nor too little. The grain in the fields and the fish in the water will not suffer from lack of rain. The days, nights, months and years will be clearly defined. The devatā who are the guardians of homes and of the city will take good care since they respect and honor rulers who are righteous. When there are rulers who are not righteous the rain and water will go wrong. The plowing will be ruined from lack of rain. The fruits and plants which grow from the earth will lose their nutritive essence and delicious taste. The tree trunks that grow will lose their healthy look. The sun, wind, the moon and stars will not regulate the seasons in the normal way. This is because the rulers do not follow the Dhamma.
>
> (Frank E. & Mai B. Reynolds [Ed./Tr.], 1982, p. 75)

Science and Buddhism

It has already been observed that Buddhism is science-friendly. The Buddha's line of inquiry conforms to the scientific method of investigation, evidence, proof, and conclusion. The very process of developing a form of Humanistic Buddhism, applicable across many cultures in the modern world, results from the encouragement of the Buddha to develop new approaches, methods and modalities.

It is equally true that science has become Buddhism-friendly. Three recent developments need to be discussed. The first is on the concept of rebirth which is intrinsic to the Buddhist ethical system based on Karma, and skillful and unskillful action. The ability to recall one's own as well as others' previous lives has been recorded as one of the attainments in the process of enlightenment. There are occasionally rare persons who at various stages of their lives — mostly while they are still uninhibited children — recall events and experiences of their previous lives. Some speak languages they had never learnt or even heard of in this life. Others recite long texts in foreign languages at a very tender age. What is extremely significant is that such people come from all parts of the world and belong to cultures where the concept of rebirth or reincarnation is not a part of their belief system.

Ian Stevenson of University of Virginia (USA) collected information on nearly 2000 such cases. He subjected each case to stringent scrutiny, looking for the slightest evidence to connect proffered information with a possible source: e.g. a story heard or read, a traveler's tale, a book or a newspaper article; a radio or television broadcast or even a fertile imagination. He was so stringent in his criteria that he succeeded in rejecting all but twenty cases on the basis of his unyielding scientific criteria. The accepted cases came from India (7 cases), Sri Lanka (3), Brazil (2), Alaska (7) and Lebanon (1). His super-critical objectivity has enabled these to be presented as "Twenty Cases Suggestive of Reincarnation" (Ian Stevenson, 1974). That rebirth is a dogma to be taken on faith has never been the Buddhist position. But to have the support of a scientifically conducted inquiry is no doubt an advantage.

Similarly illustrative of science being Buddhism-friendly is the evidence which scientific investigations have brought forth with regard to benefits of meditation and the relevance of Buddhist psychology in psychotherapy. After a systematic study of recent and on-going research on these two aspects, Padmal de Silva has the following to say:

> "In present-day psychotherapy, mindfulness meditation has also been successfully used for the dermatological condition of psoriasis which is known to have a psychological contribution (e.g.

Kabat-Zinn, Wheeler, Light, Skillings, Scharf, Cropley, Hosmer & Bernhard, 1998). It has also been used, in a well-controlled clinical trial, for anxiety (Kabat-Zinn, Massion, Kristeller, Peterson, Fletcher, Pbert, Linderkin & Santorelli, 1992). Even more important is a very recent development, involving well-established clinical psychologists in three centres — Cambridge in England, Bangor in Wales, and Toronto in Canada. The researchers, Teasdale, Williams and Segal, have been conducting a trial of mindfulness meditation to see whether this intervention will reduce the chances of relapse in patients who have recovered from depression. Those who recover from depression with treatment have a high probability of suffering further episodes of clinical depression, so reducing relapse rates is a challenge to the clinician. These researchers have compared a group of recovered depressives engaging in mindfulness practice, with a second group with no such intervention but receiving the usual psychiatric and medical follow-up. Up to now, data from 145 subjects has shown that mindfulness meditation does indeed lead to a reduction in relapse. This is a major finding in the content of present day psychiatry and psychology. A theoretical discussion of the rationale behind this work is provided by Teasdale (1999).

The point here is that the nature of the meditational endeavour, and its results as part of a Buddhist's self-development, suggest a useful role for it in the remediation for certain psychological disorders, especially stress-related ones, and also for the psychological aspects of certain physical conditions. The available clinical literature provides favourable evidence." (Padmal de Silva, 2000, pp. 174-175)

> Buddhist psychology is relevant to mental health in today's world in two obvious ways. First, it has techniques and strategies which can be used for the remediation, or therapy, of disordered or maladaptive behaviour and emotions. In other words, it has much to offer for the treatment of psychological problems. Second, it has techniques, as well as an overall stance, that can help in the prophylaxis — i.e. prevention — of psychological disorders. Prevention of psychological disorders is acknowledged as a legitimate aim of psychotherapy. In the sense that preventive work does not deal with existing aberrations, but enables a person to become less vulnerable to such aberrations and disorders, this can be seen as a higher-order aim of psychotherapy. (Ibid, p. 170)

To this may also be added the mounting medical evidence in favor of the role of prayer, positive thinking and meditation by others on critically sick persons. Remarkable results are recorded even when the sick person is not aware that others were making fervent wishes for his or her recovery. Early Buddhism has reference to a practice recommended by the Buddha himself. It is called *Saccakiriya*, meaning "truth-action" and involves wishes or resolutions phrased as: "By the power of this truth, may the following happen." Usually a discourse of the Buddha is recited and its truth is invoked for somebody's health or success. This is the basis for the chanting of *Paritta* (Book of Protection) in Southern Buddhism. Scientific inquiry has begun to establish the efficacy of such practices, which had hitherto been belief-based.

To this one may also add that quantum mechanics and the uncertainty principle are posited by scientists as confirmation of the Buddhist doctrines of impermanence and no-self. How science contributes to the understanding of Buddhism is a continuing research theme among scholars.

Comprehending Inter-working

A Renewed Wine in a Redesigned Bottle

When the Grand Master Hsing Yun urges us to comprehend the inter-workings of societies, science, economics, and the environment, he sees the relevance and usefulness of two intertwined processes:

(i) Using the insights in the Buddha's teachings to formulate the Buddhist standards, norms and positions on current issues and to contribute with conviction to the growing concepts of social justice, equity and human rights and universal ethics; and

(ii) Utilizing the scientific support to Buddhist beliefs and practices to strengthen the intellectual and popular acceptance of the Buddha's teachings as relevant to modern life.

On the whole, Buddhism has an advantage which no other religion has. It begins with "thing as they really are." The term used in Pali is "*yathābhūtañāna*" — the knowledge of things as they are. As changes take place in society, our knowledge of society, too, changes. Solutions once applicable to a given problem cannot be equally efficacious at all times. Therefore no rule can be valid for ever. A very interesting example of the Buddha's understanding of this phenomenon comes from the rules of discipline for the monastics. When the Sangha was founded, he did not begin by laying down rules and regulations for everything. In fact, there were no formal rules during the first twenty years of his mission.

Rules were formulated in response to situations. Each rule was made when an incident demanding regulation took place. It is also the reason why many aspects of monastic life are not covered by rules of discipline. The same is true of social norms. No straight-forward answers are to be found in Buddhist literature in general for such present-day issues as abortion, euthanasia, suicide, genetic engineering etc. within the scope of bioethics. This could be a weakness in any religious system but not in Buddhism.

The Buddha sought and taught principles which applied to problem-solving in general. He trusted in the human being's capacity to think and to think critically. He identified intention or volition (*cetanā*) as the morally significant prelude to every thought, word or deed. Ethical significance or morality was judged as skillful or unskillful (*akusala* or *kusala*) in relation to assuring or denying the good of the many and the happiness of the many (*bahujanahitāya, bahujanasukhāya*). Each generation could, therefore, address the issues of the time with these broad principles. As a result Buddhism grew and expanded. It met the needs of different cultures. It has remained one but yet become many.

The growth of Buddhism into diverse traditions, schools or sects is a sign of its flexibility and ever-renewing relevance to life. New thoughts are explored. Refreshingly cogent conclusions are drawn. Neither metaphors of new wine in old bottles or old wine in new bottles would apply to this process. The Buddhists in general give equal emphasis to the newness of both the contents and the package. A renewed wine in a redesigned bottle would be a more appropriate metaphor.

A Flexibility Leading to Timelessness

Two examples could be cited from Mahāyāna scriptures pertaining to a layman and a laywoman. In *Vimalakīrtinirdesasūtra*, the Buddha is said to explain what a Buddha-field of a Bodhisattva is. He says that it is related to the Bodhisattva's involvement in "the development of living beings," "the discipline of the living beings," "increasing their holy spiritual faculties," and "aims of living beings."

In what follows are given as many as eighteen definitions of the Buddha-field and each opens up a new vista of action relevant to the world of the living:

- A field of positive thought, where living beings **free of hypocrisy and deceit** will be born.
- A field of high resolve, where living beings who have harvested **the two stores and have planted the roots of virtue** will be born.
- The magnificence of the conception of the spirit of enlightenment, where living beings who are actually **participating in the Mahāyāna** will be born.
- A field of generosity, where living beings who **give away all their possessions** will be born.
- A field of morality, where living beings who follow **the path of the ten virtues with positive thoughts** will be born.
- A field of tolerance, where living beings with **the transcendences of tolerance, discipline, and the superior trance** will be born.
- A field of effort, where living beings who devote **efforts to virtue** will be born.
- A field of meditation, where living beings who are **evenly balanced through mindfulness and awareness** will be born.
- A field of wisdom, where living beings who are **destined for the ultimate** will be born.
- A field of the four immeasurables, where living beings who **live by love, compassion, joy, and impartiality** will be born.

- A field of the four unifications, where living beings who are **held together by all the liberations** will be born.
- A field of skill in liberative technique of enlightenment, where living beings **skilled in all liberative techniques and activities** will be born.
- A field consisting of the thirty-seven aids to enlightenment where living beings who devote their efforts to **the four foci of mindfulness, the four right efforts, the four bases of magical power, the five spiritual faculties, the five strengths, the seven factors of enlightenment, and the eight branches of the holy path** will be born.
- A Bodhisattva's mind of total dedication, where **the ornaments of all virtues** will appear.
- The doctrine that eradicates the eight adversities, so that **the three bad migrations** will cease, and there will be no such thing as the eight adversities.
- A field consisting of **personal observance of the basic precepts and restraints in blaming others for their transgressions**, where even the word 'crime' will never be mentioned.
- The purity of the path of the ten virtues, in which living beings who are **secure in long life, great in wealth, chaste in conduct, enhanced by true speech, soft-spoken, free of divisive intrigues and adroit in reconciling factions, enlightening in their conversations, free of envy, free of malice, and endowed with perfect views** will be born.

(Robert A.F. Thurman [Tr.], 1976, pp. 16-18)

As the words emphasized show, what this list highlights through this special form of presentation are the basic Buddhist ethical values. In *Śrīmālāsiṃhanādasūtra* are listed the following ten vows which, in a similar manner, stress thoughts, words and action which one has to avoid:

(1) I shall not permit any **thought of violating morality**.
(2) I shall not allow any **thought of disrespect toward the teachers** (*guru*).
(3) I shall not allow any **thought of anger and ill will toward sentient beings**.
(4) I shall not allow any **thought of jealousy toward the glory of others and the perfections of others.**
(5) I shall not allow any **thought of covetousness, no matter how meager the donated food**.
(6) I shall not **accumulate wealth for my own use**, but shall deal with it to assist the poor and friendless.
(7) With the four articles of conversion, I shall benefit the sentient beings and **not convert them for my own sake**; indeed, I shall seek to convert the sentient beings with **my mind unoccupied with material things, ever unsatisfied, and not retreating.**
(8) When in the future, I observe sentient beings who are friendless, trapped and bound, diseased, troubled, poor and miserable, I shall **not forsake them for a single moment until they are restored**. I shall liberate them from each of those sufferings; having conferred goods upon them, I shall leave them.
(9) When I see persons with **sinful occupations such as dealing in pigs, and those who violate the Doctrine and Discipline proclaimed by the Tathagata, I shall not take it lightly**; and wherever my residence in towns, villages, cities, districts, and capitals, I shall destroy what should be destroyed and shall foster what should be fostered.
(10) Having embraced the Illustrious Doctrine, I shall **not forget it even in a single thought**. (Alex Wayman and Hideko Wayman [Tr.], 1990, pp. 64-66)

Both these are excellent regroupings of the many teachings of the Buddha. They are presented in conformity with the growing concepts of Mahāyāna Buddhism. Authenticity of the contents is beyond question. It is the selection and presentation which contribute to its relevance to the target audience.

Such instances of re-emphasis found in the vast Buddhist literature in Pali, Sanskrit, Chinese, Tibetan and many other Asian national languages illustrate how a similar process could make Buddhism relevant to a given time or situation, by comprehending the inter-working of all interacting subsystems of the social system. This is how Buddhism has grown and assumed a great measure of "Timelessness" (*akālika*). Having no dogma to defend or conform to, scholars and writers have exercised their many-sided creativity in this process.

Clarity of Vision and Good Planning

The Path of the Arahant and the Bodhisattva Way

The Grand Master's overarching plea is that Buddhism should be developed into a viable religion by adapting it to today's conditions. The process he suggests for this is to make choices just as we had seen in the Srimālās ten vows and Vimalakīrti's definitions of the Buddha-field. He advises us to make such choices on "clear reasoning and good intentions." He takes as examples the two major traditions of Buddhism for the importance that has to be placed on "clarity of vision and good planning," namely:

- The Path of the Arahant with its Four Directions (or Paths = Pali *Magga*) and Four Fruits (Pali *Phala*); and
- The Bodhisattva Way of Mahāyāna, divided into fifty-two detailed stages.

Our discussions so far have amply demonstrated that methodical reasoning based on clear-cut intentions has been the hallmark of Buddhism. There has been nothing haphazard in the Buddha's teachings nor in their adaptations by different traditions, schools and sects.

One has only to examine the structure and the flow of a Nikāya or Āgama discourse to see how the intentions evolved into a clear vision and the presentation emerged from good planning. For example, the very first discourse, *Dhammacakkappavattanasutta*, is organized on a strictly pedagogical plan. The vision of the Buddha was to save humanity from suffering. After six years of study, experimentation and reflection, he had found the Way to the End of Suffering. Addressing the five one-time companions in meditation, who left him when he abandoned the course of self-mortification, the Buddha addressed the first point of discord between him and his audience. "There are two extremes to be avoided by one who aspires for higher spiritual attainments." Having had their attention with that opening statement, he proceeded to his attention-retaining method of enumerating what was to follow: "There are four Noble Truths" and "The Path consists of eight factors or strands." Each truth was concisely defined. The definition of *Dukkha* as comprising eight empirically testable situations is a remarkable exercise in logical sequencing. What had to be done with each Noble Truth was lucidly stated: The first has to be understood; the second abandoned; the third attained and the fourth followed. At the end of the session, however only one out of five fulfilled the objective of the discourse.

As a conscientious and determined teacher, the Buddha must have reviewed his lesson plan thoroughly. The proof of such a revision comes out of the structure of the second discourse: *Anatta-lakkhaṇasutta*. This time he began with *Anicca* (Sanskrit *Anitya*) or impermanence resulting from constant and unpredictable change as the starting point of the presentation. How very systematically he argued that impermanence led to unsatisfactoriness and misery and the two characteristics together should convince anyone that there was no permanent, unchanging entity to be identified as, "This is mine. This is I. This is my Self." No doubt, the second lesson plan was more successful. The other four in the audience also attained enlightenment and resulting liberation.

Another striking example of a carefully structured discourse is *Mahāsatipaṭṭhānasutta* (D. 22, M.10) on the Four Foundations of

Mindfulness. Its attention-catching statement is "This is **the sole way** leading to purification of beings, to passing far beyond grief and lamentation, to the eradication of suffering and misery, to the attainment of the right method, and to the realization of Nirvāṇa." (*Ekāyano ayaṃ maggo*). Again, each section begins by giving the number of factors or elements to be immediately discussed. Each factor or element is then presented for review and reinforcement. Here the Buddha's method of revision was not a mechanical repetition. Instead, he would ask the learners to apply what was taught in three situations:

(i) as applied to one's own self (*ajjhatta*);
(ii) as applied to others (*bahiddha*); and
(iii) as applied to both oneself and others (*ajjhatta-bahiddha*).

As the Grand Master Hsing Yun points out, the Path leading to the End of Suffering, as described by the Buddha, does exemplify clarity of vision and good planning. The process of self-improvement and mental cultivation begins with coming to know the message of the Buddha and deciding to seek deliverance from suffering. One would choose the life of a monastic as more convenient for one's spiritual purpose and renounce the comforts and pleasures of lay life. As one proceeds there are Five Obstacles to overcome. Meditating on specified subjects, one represses on an interim basis (*vikkhambhanapahāna*) lust, malice, sloth and torpor, restlessness and worry, and skepticism or doubt. With further meditation and concentration of the mind, one reaches the point of entering the Path of *Sotāpatti*[21] (Stream-entry). The effort at this stage is to eradicate three basic defilements or fetters: namely,

1. Self-view (*sakkāyadiṭṭhi*), i.e. the illusory view that one's self is permanent and unchanging and, therefore, one is justified in being self-important, self-centered and selfish.

[21] The four Paths and Fruits are frequently mentioned in Mahāyāna Sutras. Some translators prefer to retain the Sanskrit terminology as *Śrotāpatti* or *Śrotāpanna*, *Sakṛdāgāmin*, *Anāgāmin* and *Arhant*.

2. Reliance on mere ritual (*sīlabbataparāmāsa*), i.e. the wrong belief that rites and ritual would lead one to liberation. (Eradicating this belief leads one to the realization that one has to work diligently for one's liberation through Right Thought, Right Motive, Right Speech, Right Action, Right Livelihood, Right Effort, Right Mindfulness and Right Concentration of the Mind).
3. Perplexity (*vicikicchā*) arising out of doubts on the efficacy of the Path.

Once these three defilements or fetters are removed, one is established in the Fruit of Stream-entry (*Sotāpattiphala*). When this stage was reached, one would attain liberation within seven rebirths.

One proceeded from here to the Path of Once-Returner (*sakadāgāmi*) to suppress

4. Lust for sensual pleasures (*kāmarāga*).
5. Malice (*vyāpāda*) which includes anger, aversion, animosity, hatred and illwill.

With the suppression of these defilments or fetters was reached the Fruit of Once-Returner, after which one returned only once to human existence to be liberated.

The next effort is to eradicate the same two fetters through the Path of Non-Returner (*Anāgāmi*). Once this was achieved, one attained the Fruit of Non-Returner and would be liberated from one of the Brahma-worlds without returning to human state.

Hence entering the Path of Arahant, one proceeds to eradicate the remaining five defilements or fetters:

6. Desire for Corporeal or Fine-Material existence (*Rūparāga*) (i.e. in a Brahama-world with form)
7. Desire for Non-Material existence (i.e. in a Brahma-world without form)
8. Conceit (*Māna*)
9. Restlessness (*Uddhacca*)
10. Ignorance or non-knowledge (*Avijjā*)

Once these are eradicated, the process to the ending of suffering begins as spelled out in the twelve links of the Dependent Origination (*Paṭiccasamuppāda*, Sanskrit *Pratītyasamutpāda*):

Without *Ignorance* (*Avijjā*), Mental Formulations or Volitional Activities cease.

Without *Mental Formulations or Volitional Activities* (*Sankhārā*), Consciousness ceases.

Without *Consciousness* (*Viññāṇa*), Mental and Physical Phenomena cease.

Without *Mental and Physical Phenomena* (*Nāma-rūpa*), Six Sense organs (i.e., including mind) cease.

Without *Six Sense organs* (*Saḷāyatana*), Contact with the External World ceases.

Without *Contact with the External World* (*Phassa*), Feeling ceases.

Without *Feeling* (*Vedanā*), Craving ceases.

Without *Craving* (*Taṇhā*), Clinging ceases.

Without *Clinging* (*Upādāna)*, the Process of Becoming ceases.

Without *The Process of Becoming* (*Bhava*), Birth (or Rebirth) ceases.

Without *Birth* (or *Rebirth*) (*Jāti*), Old Age and Death and all forms of suffering (*Jarā-Maraṇa*) cease.

With the ceasing of *Bhava* (the process of Becoming), the process of rebirth stops and one reaches Nibbāṇa, the End of Suffering.

As the Grand Master Hsing Yun explains, this is the Path of the Arahant. That it is a planned process of self-perfection is quite clear. It is a path of ethical development and Sarvapalli Radhakrishnan, an eminent exponent of Indian philosophy, was impressed by its success:

> "The elevated morality taught by Buddha, that only the pure in heart shall attain salvation, sums up the Law and the Prophets. Buddha justified the practice of the good even to those who did not believe in a personal God. No other independent ethics ever thundered into our ears the majesty of

> the good. It is the flaming ideal of righteousness that helped Buddhism to succeed as a religion... Buddhism succeeded so well because it was a religion of love, giving voice to all the inarticulate forces which were working against the established order and ceremonial religion, addressing itself to the poor, the lowly and the disinherited.
>
> (*Radhakrishnan*, 1966, p. 63)

The Mahāyāna Bodhisattva Way is another plan for self-perfection with the dual objectives of saving others and achieving liberation. One has only to read Śāntideva's *Bodhicaryāvatāra* (sometimes called *Bodhisattvacaryāvatāra*) to experience the sheer depth of fervent dedication of a Bodhisattva to serving others:

May I be the doctor and medicine
And may I be the nurse
For all sick beings in the world
Until everyone is healed (III, 8)

May a rain of food and drink descend
To clear away the pain of thirst and hunger
And during the aeon of famine
May I myself change into food and drink (9)

May I become an inexhaustible treasure
For those who are poor and destitute;
May I turn into all things they could need
And may these be placed beside them (10)

May all who say bad things to me
Or cause me any other harm
And those who mock and insult me
Have the fortune to fully awaken (17)

May I be an island to those who seek one
And a lamp for those desiring light
May I be a bed for all who wish to rest

And a slave for all who want a slave (19)

(Steven Batchelor [Tr.], 1979, pp. 23 & 25)

The division of the Bodhisattva Way into fifty-two detailed stages[22] is cited by the Grand Master as another example of clarity of vision and good planning. They are described first in terms of groups and are enumerated as follows:

52 Marvelous enlightenment = Buddhahood

51 Equal enlightenment = enlightenment equal to a Buddha but yet a Bodhisattva

41-50 Ten Stages (*Daśabhūmi*), namely, Joy (*pramuditā*), freedom from defilement (*vimalā*), emission of light (*prabhākārī*), glowing wisdom (*arcismati*), overcoming the difficult (*sudurjaya*), manifestation of reality (*abhimukhi*), far-reaching (*dūrangamā*), immovable (*acalā*), wondrous wisdom (*sādhumatī*) and Dharma-cloud (*Dharmamegha*).

31-40 Ten Dedications of Merit, namely, dedication to saving all beings without any mental image of sentient beings, indestructible dedication, dedication equal to all Buddhas, dedication reaching all places, dedication of inexhaustible treasuries of merit, dedication causing all roots of goodness to endure, dedication equally adapting all sentient beings, dedication with the character of thusness, unbound liberated dedication, and boundless dedication equal to the cosmos.

21-30 The Ten Practices, namely, giving joy, beneficial practice, non-opposition, indo-

[22] The Japanese *Bosatsu Yōraku Hongo Sutra* and the Tendai text *Hokke Gengi* describe these fifty-two stages: Dictionnaire du Bouddhisme, Editions Rocher, Paris 1991, pp. 84-85.

mitability (= unsurpassed energy), non-confusion, skillful manifestation, non-attachment, practice of what is difficult to attain, good teachings, and truth.

11-20 Ten Abidings, namely, awakening operation, nurturing, practice, producing virtues, expedient means, correct mind, no back-sliding, true *chīd* (i.e. deluded views do not arise and awakening does not cease), Dharma-prince (i.e. being assured of becoming a future Buddha), and anointment (sprinkling water on the head).

1-10 Ten Faiths, namely, faith, mindfulness, endeavor, mental stability, wisdom of understanding emptiness, pure self-restraint, returning of merit, maintaining Dharma within oneself, detachment and aspiration.

(Charles Muller, *Dictionary of East Asian Buddhist Terms.* http://www.human.toyogakuen-u.ac.jp)

Even without definitions of each of the terms listed, it is clear that the fifty-two stages of the Bodhisattva Way represent a progressive course of spiritual development. It starts with faith and culminates in the attainment of the Buddhahood. Each stage reflects essential Buddhist virtues which are upheld by all traditions.

Both the Path of the Arahant and the Bodhisattva Way are characteristic of the systematic approach to spiritual progress. In both, the vision of enlightenment and the pursuit of a planned process are clearly defined and the Grand Master is justified in upholding them as examples of the Buddhist clarity of vision and good planning.

Universal Buddhism for Social Well-being

Humanistic Buddhism as conceived by the Grand Master Hsing Yun is a form of Universal Buddhism. His pragmatic approach to evolving a set of values, insights and moral standards for people to "live fully, virtuously and compassionately in this world" is based on two courses of action:

(i) Scan the entirety of spiritual and ethical values and insights of all Buddhist traditions, schools and sects and choose and synthesize in the form of Humanistic Buddhism those which are relevant to modern life; and

(ii) Place equal emphasis on divergent Buddhist practices ranging from the repetition of a formula or chanting of scriptures to intensive meditation in isolation but with the determination that service to others must go hand-in-hand with self-cultivation.

When it comes to the rich and varied heritage of World Buddhism, the Grand Master excludes nothing, ignores nothing and does not glorify or degrade anything. His tolerance of Buddhist practices of diverse types is remarkable.

In those who mechanically turn a prayer-wheel or a prayer-drum the Grand Master recognizes the depth of piety. In the repetition of such formulas as "*Namu amida-budsu*", "*Namo amito fo*" "*Namu myo-horenge-kyo*" or "*Om maṇi padme huṃ*," he sees the value of a focused mind concentrating on the Buddha and his teachings. In chanting of every tradition, he sees the virtue of congregational participation in worship and the spiritual dimensions of such experience. In Five Precept Retreats and similar exercises in spiritual development, he sees the zenith of commitment. In the life of a monastic he sees ultimate fulfillment.

He upholds virtue or morality (*sīla*), concentration of the mind (*samādhi*) and wisdom (*paññā* Sanskrit *Prajñā*) as the triple training for spiritual perfection. In his latest book, *Lotus in the Stream*, he says,

> "Buddhist practice must start with who we are and what we do. First we learn to control the negative impulses of our bodies. This is morality. Then we learn to control our minds. This is meditation. Then we learn to understand the deep truths of life. This is wisdom. Each stage depends on the one

before it... Meditation is an essential part of Buddhist practice, but no one should think that meditation is all that there is to Buddhism... Meditation is a door; what goes through the door is our compassion for others.

The biggest single reason that people leave Buddhism or fail to gain very much from their practice of it is that they have not learned how to foster in themselves a proper balance between their experience of the Buddha's teachings and their understanding of those teachings... The purpose of chanting and meditating is to show us that the insights of Shakyamuni Buddha are *real*. When we experience them in meditation, or when we are inspired by them in chanting, we renew ourselves and empower ourselves to continue the long process of introspection and moral growth that is the path to enlightenment." (pp. 14-15)

Further, he says in the same book,

"Humanistic Buddhism is not a new kind of Buddhism; it is simply a name used to emphasize the core teachings of the Buddha. The Buddha taught wisdom and compassion. These teachings always lead us back to the lives of other sentient beings. To not understand the unity of human nature and Buddha nature is to not understand the teachings of the Buddha. Humanistic Buddhism encourages us to participate in the world and to be a source of energy that is beneficial to others. Our enlightenment depends on others, just as their enlightenment depends on us... The oneness of all life and the unity of all life inspire us to participate in life. All of us must recognize that we are needed by others. By serving others we serve ourselves. By recognizing the Buddha in others, we learn to find him in ourselves.

> I could say many things about humanistic Buddhism, but it would probably be best for me to sum it up by discussing the principle virtues of the bodhisattva path: the six *paramitas*. The six *paramitas* are the perfect guide to humanistic Buddhism, as they are to all Buddhist practice. They teach us how to fulfill our humanity as we discover the Buddha within. The six *paramitas* teach us how to discover the truth by balancing our thoughts and our actions, our wisdom and our compassion, our transcendental awareness and our awareness of the relative truths of the phenomenal universe." (p. 154)

So very comprehensive and all-embracing is the Grand Master's concept and interpretation of Humanistic Buddhism. Social well-being is its primary goal.

Conclusion

The foregoing chapters have been organized and written as an explanatory commentary on Grand Master Hsing Yun's inspiring and informative message to the First International Conference on Humanistic Buddhism. To the extent permitted by time and space are analyzed the salient features of Buddhism — with special reference to the teachings of Śākyamuni Buddha, as reflected in the Southern Buddhist Canon in Pali and corresponding Āgama Sūtras in Chinese.

The more we examine what the Grand Master presents as his concept and interpretation of Humanistic Buddhism in the light of traditional teachings, the more we are convinced that

- Buddhism, as it is practiced worldwide, is an enormously rich and varied spiritual, religious and philosophical heritage of humanity;
- the Grand Master Hsing Yun has blazed a new trail in underscoring the importance of benefiting from the diversity of Buddhist traditions; and
- in doing so, he has become an illustrious symbol of unity for all Buddhist traditions.

As the Grand Master has himself clarified on several occasions, Humanistic Buddhism is not a new form of Buddhism. It is neither a schism nor a new church. Nor is it a gimmick; nor a play on words. Śākyamuni Buddha was himself human and most of his teachings were addressed to real human beings — the people of the street. The Grand Master has been inspired by the humanistic overtones and considerations in the Buddha's teachings.

As a teenager he was impressed by the enthusiasm of a senior Buddhist activist of China, namely Master Taixu, whose cry was to bring Buddhism, literally and metaphorically, from the mountains to the city and the village. With well-defined study, research, reflection, consultation and discussion, Grand Master Hsing Yun has identified the most significant mission of Buddhism in the modern world. His vision of this mission is that Buddhism has to serve humanity as a whole. A practicing Buddhist has to give equal attention to serving others as to perfecting oneself for eventual liberation.

What emerges from his many writings and speeches is a simple but yet profound definition of Humanistic Buddhism. That is, whatever be the tradition of Buddhism, it becomes Humanistic Buddhism when it is conceived and practiced with the main purpose of ensuring social well-being. To tie this definition with the title of this book, one may say "**Buddhism for Social Well-being or Socially Engaged Buddhism is Humanistic Buddhism**."

The many citations from relevant scriptures of both Southern and Northern Buddhism establish the authenticity of the Grand Master's line of an argument. Even the most puritanical partisan to a particular tradition, school or sect would recognize that the Grand Master has succeeded in

- convincing us of the universality of Buddhism and the intrinsic unity which underlies the apparent diversity; and
- persuading us to join hands in a common, concerted effort to overcome prejudice, bigotry and intolerance.

The goal of Universal Buddhism is most likely to be achieved through Humanistic Buddhism.

The Grand Master expresses — especially in action — his appreciation of Śākyamuni Buddha's pragmatism. Hence does he confine his efforts to the knowable and the doable. Under his directions, such organs of implementation of Humanistic Buddhism, as the Fo Guang Shan Buddhist Order, Buddha's Light International Association, temples, universities, colleges, schools and media enterprises, are not only guided by clear goals of service to humanity but also action-oriented. The efficiency and effectiveness of these organs stem from the practical orientation, which is an essential element of Humanistic Buddhism, as interpreted by Grand Master Hsing Yun.

One would also see from the foregoing analysis that the Grand Master's basic concern is in re-ordering the priority that people tend to assign in their spiritual or religious life. If he downplays self-cultivation in preference to altruistic service, his intention is to highlight what appears to be more important for a religious person today. The Grand Master sees a world in which seventy percent of the human population lives in poverty, illiteracy and ignorance, with hunger and malnutrition, disease and morbidity, social inequalities and exploitation dangerously on the rise. He is conscious that the greed for immediate gains and pleasures has over-exploited and abused the environment to a degree that the very survival of the humankind as well as life in all its forms is threatened. His concept of compassion and wisdom is that saving those in the human realm is the most urgent and appropriate way to translate into action these two Buddhist ideals.

No one can disagree with him when he shows that every single one of the six Pāramitās in the Mahāyāna tradition (and certainly the ten Pāramitās of Southern Buddhism) can and should be fulfilled in this very life. The fundamental crux of Humanistic Buddhism is that the social well-being of all and sundry is the foundation for all Buddhist practices which include the mastery of sacred scriptures, ritualistic chanting, living a virtuous life, retreats, development of mindfulness, meditation, and realization of wisdom.

One more conclusion emerges from our study of the Grand Master's interpretation of Humanistic Buddhism. That is, his primary concern is not with theory but with purposeful, well-directed action. He is a man of action, a planner, a strategist and an organization man *par excellence*. He is a visionary but yet not a dreamer. So to him Humanistic Buddhism is not another textbook version of Buddhism. Instead he sees it as a process in which the conscientization of Buddhists and friends of Buddhism is the first step. What is meant by conscientization is more or less the same process that the famous Brazilian adult educator, Paulo Friere, advocated for the oppressed sections of society to assume responsibility for their destiny. The Grand Master urges Buddhists not to be passive, inactive slaves to their current lot. They must create the conditions leading to their destiny rather than succumb to prevailing conditions, he says emphatically. Once this awareness is generated, a sea change is bound to result.

The Grand Master also has a vision of the agents who would initiate and manage this change. His confidence in the Sangha as the foremost among change-agents is significant. The Sangha has proved its mettle by twenty-six centuries of survival, expansion, and active service. It is also the most fundamental Buddhist institution which, in its rules, procedures, values and structures, has remained cohesive and uniform irrespective of doctrinal, ritualistic, and observational diversity. With equal emphasis the Grand Master spells out the role of the laity, the scholar and the student. The laity have progressively become an intellectual force in the promotion of Buddhism, besides continuing the traditional role of material supporters. They are increasingly seeking spiritual direction and guidance from the Sangha and the need for closer cooperation between them is vital.

More eloquent than all exhortations are the steps which the Grand Master has taken to prepare all these change-agents for the tasks ahead. Humanistic Buddhism is about people. His concrete actions for the advancement and benefit of people through education and social services speak louder than his words. If the efficacy of Humanistic Buddhism is borne out by selective doctrines immediately relevant to social well-being, its effectiveness is demonstrated by the most impressive religious and educational infrastructure which spans every continent of the world.

It is with an incomparable spectrum of on-hand experiences, ranging from scholarship and education to motivating millions to accept his leadership, that Grand Master Hsing Yun underscores the adoption by Buddhists of two very important management principles, namely:

- A systems approach to the solution of social problems, which, in his own words, is based on "comprehending the interworkings of societies, science, economics and the environment", and
- Clarity of vision and good planning.

His is the language of the doer, who sets for himself objectives and raises and mobilizes resources to accomplish them. The Grand Master is convinced that the teachings of the Buddha lend support to the management style which he had perfected all on his own as a by-product of every little incident in his life. His entire life, as episodes that he had chosen to illustrate his values and insights show, is a case study on ever-renewing and ever-expanding management leadership.

An adherent to Humanistic Buddhism has to be an effective manager — a person with a vision and a mission and significantly dedicated to achieving realistic objectives. As his plea in the name of Humanistic Buddhism reaches a wider audience in the world, Buddhists of all traditions, schools and sects as well as ever-increasing friends of Buddhism would turn to projects and activities for the benefit of people. Planning and implementational skills are, therefore, indispensable to them as much as the comprehension of the essential teachings of the Buddha.

The last but not the least conclusion which results from our analysis is that Grand Master Hsing Yun's lasting appeal is for all Buddhists in the world. He desires all to strive for the benefit and the good of the many harmoniously within the framework of Humanistic Buddhism. Though he is the recognized 48th Patriarch of the Linji Chan tradition, the founder-leader of the Fo Guang

Shan Buddhist Order and, thereby, a leading light of Māhayāna Buddhism, he has risen above all parochial and sectarian considerations. He treats all traditions fairly. He questions the validity or authenticity of none. He has no hesitation in seeking wisdom wherever it is found and acknowledges his readiness to quote from all traditions. The comprehensiveness of the literary sources which he relies on is by itself a laudable example.

I have on a previous occasion compared the Grand Master's Humanistic Buddhism to an umbrella under which all sects, schools and traditions of Buddhism could unite, act together, and serve humanity. This study has only redoubled my appreciation of the unifying role of Humanistic Buddhism. It is my hope and my fervent wish that the message of the Grand Master reaches the spiritual and religious leadership in the world so that the unique potential of the teachings of the Buddha to bring about the well-being of every sentient being is fully mobilized. May the Buddha's wish that every man, woman and child thinks, speaks and acts for the good of the many be fulfilled through Humanistic Buddhism, as conceived and interpreted by Venerable Grand Master Dr. Hsing Yun.

REFERENCES

Bachelor, Steven (Tr.)	1979	*A Guide to the Bodhisattva's Way of Life*, Dharmasala
Burma Pitaka Association	1985	*Guide to Tipitaka*, Pangoon
Cleary, Thomas (Tr.)	1998	*The Sutra of Hui-neng: Grand Master of Zen with Hui-neng's Commentary on the Diamond Sutra*, Boston, Shambhala
Conze, Edward (Tr.)	1973	*The Perfection of Wisdom in Eight Thousand Lines and its Summary*, Four Seasons Foundation, San Francisco
De Silva, Padmal	2000	Buddhism and Psychotherapy: The Role of Self-control Strategies, *Hsi Lai Journal of Humanistic Buddhism, HLJHB, Vol. I.*
Guruge, Ananda W.P.	1982	*Miracle of Instruction*, Lakehouse, Colombo
	1989	*Mahāvaṃsa — A New Annotated Translation With Prolegomena*, Associated Newspapers of Ceylon Limited, Colombo.
	1993	*Asoka the Righteous: A Definitive Biography*, Central

Cultural Fund, Colombo.

1993-1 *An Agenda for the International Buddhist Community*, Karunaratne and Sons, Colombo.

1999 *What in Brief is Buddhism?* Mitram, Monterey Park, CA.

2000 *Humanistic Elements in Early Buddhism and the "Theravāda Tradition," HLJHB, Vol. I.*

Humphreys, Christmas 1976 *A Popular Dictionary of Buddhism*, London/Dublin, Redwood Burn

Kabat-Zinn, J., Massion, A.O., Kristeller, J., Peterson, L.G., Fletcher, K., Pbert, L., Linderking, C.O. & Santoreli, S.F. 1992 Effectiveness of a meditation-based stress reduction program in the treatment of anxiety disorders. *American Journal of Psychiatry*, 149, 936-943.

Kabat-Zinn, J., Wheeler, E., Light, T., Skillings, A., Cropley, T., Hosmer, D. & Bernhard, J. 1998 The influence of a mindfulness-based stress reduction intervention on rates of skin clearing in patients with moderate to serve psoriasis undergoing phototherapy (UVB) and photochemotherapy

		(PUVA) *Psychosomatic Medicine*, 60, 625-63
Kawamura, Leslie (Tr.)	1975	*Golden Zephyr: Instructions From a Spiritual Friend*, Dharma Publishing, Emeryville, CA
Kimball, Richard	2000	Humanistic Buddhism as Conceived and Interpreted by Grand Master Hsing Yun of Fo Guang Shan, *HLJHB, Vol. I.*
Long, Darui	2000	Humanistic Buddhism From Venerable Tai Xu to Grand Master Hsing Yun, *HLJHB, Vol. I.*
	2000-1	The Interfaith Dialogues Between Tai Xu and Christians in the 1930s, *Buddhist-Christian Studies*, Harvard-Yenching Institute
Nānamoli, Bhikkhu	1972	*The Life of Buddha — as it Appears in the Pali Canon, the Oldest Authentic Record*, Buddhist Publication Society, Kandy
Radhakrishnan, Sarvapalli	1966	*Indian Philosophy Vols. I & II*, George Allen & Union, London
Reynolds, Frank E. and	1982	*Traibhūmikathā,* Berkeley, Asian Humanities

Mai B. (Tr.)		
Stevenson, Ian	1974	*Twenty Cases Suggestive of Reincarnation*, Univ. Press of Virginia, Charlottesville
Teasdale J.	1999	Megacognition, Mindfulness and the Modification of Mood Disorders, *Psychology and Psychotherapy 6.*
Thich Huyen-Vi	1971	*A Critical Study of the Life and Works of Sāriputta Thera*, Linh Son Research Institute, Joinville-le-Pont (France)
Thurman, Robert A. F. (Tr.)	1976	*The Holy Teachings of Vimalakīrti, A Mahāyāna Scripture*, Pennsylvania University Press, University Park and London
Wayman, Alex and Wayman, Hideko (Tr.)	1990	*The Lion's Roar of Queen Śrimālā, A Buddhist Scripture on the Tathāgatagarbha Theory*, Motilal Banarsidass, Delhi,

ABBREVIATIONS

A	*Anguttaranikāya*
Cv	*Cullavagga*
D	*Dīghanikāya*
Dp	*Dhammapada*
It	*Itivuttaka*
M	*Majjhimanikāya*
Mt	*Majjhimanikāya Commentary*
Mv	*Mahāvagga*
Pac	*Pācittiya in Suttavibhanga*
S	*Saṃyuttanikāya*
Sn	*Suttanipāta*
Sv	*Suttavibhanga*
U	*Udāna*